A GUIDE F[...] CHANGING BODIES

Boys Puberty Book Ages 8-12

AUTHOR
DIANE POPE

Copyright Page

Title: A guide for boys about changing bodies

Sub Title: Boys Puberty Book Ages 8-12

Author: Diane Pope

Published by Skilled Fun

SKILLED FUN

For permission requests, contact the publisher:

Skilled Fun

401 Ryland Street,

Suite 200-A,

Reno, NV, 89502,

USA

ISBN: 979-8-89256-157-0

Printed in USA

CONTENTS

SPECIAL BONUS

Want this bonus book for free?

SKILLS and be the first to claim a free
download of our upcoming releases.

Scan the
QR CODE

Join
Today!

INTRODUCTION

Welcome to "A Guide for Boys About Changing Bodies." Whether you're just dipping your toes into the waters of puberty or riding the waves of hormonal changes, this book is your trusty compass, guiding you through the wild and wonderful journey of growing up.

Now, let's get real for a moment – puberty can be like embarking on a grand expedition into uncharted territory. Your body is gearing up for some major transformations, and it's normal to feel excitement, confusion, and maybe even a touch of apprehension. But fear not, brave explorers! We're here to be your seasoned guides, offering insights, advice, and a healthy dose of humor along the way.

In these pages, you'll find everything you need to know about the fascinating world of changing bodies. From the mysterious workings of hormones to the ins and outs of physical and emotional shifts, consider this book your ultimate survival guide for navigating the ups and downs of puberty.

But hey, this isn't your typical stuffy instruction manual – oh no! We're here to make learning about your body fun and engaging. So, expect plenty of jokes, quirky illustrations, and relatable stories to keep you entertained as you embark on this epic quest of self-discovery.

1

WELCOME TO THE JOURNEY: EMBRACING CHANGE

Welcome, young adventurers, to an incredible journey – the journey of growing up! As you embark on this exciting path, you'll encounter many changes, both inside and out. This book is here to guide you through this journey of puberty, helping you understand the transformations happening to your body and mind.

Puberty is a natural and normal part of growing up; every boy goes through it at his own pace. Some changes might happen quickly, while others may take a little longer – and that's perfectly okay! The important thing to remember is that you're not alone. Many boys your age are experiencing the same things, and plenty of people are here to support you along the way, including your parents, teachers, and even friends.

During puberty, your body goes through a series of changes as it prepares for adulthood. You might start noticing that you're growing taller, your muscles might become stronger, and your voice might deepen. You may also start to develop hair in new places, like on your face, under your arms, and around your genitals. These changes can feel strange or even a little uncomfortable initially, but they're all a natural part of growing up.

Along with physical changes, you might also notice changes happening inside of you. You might start having new feelings and emotions you haven't experienced before. You might feel more curious about the world around you, or you might start to feel attracted to people differently. These feelings are all a normal part of growing up, and they're nothing to be ashamed of.

It's important to remember that everyone's journey through puberty is unique, and there's no right or wrong way to experience it. Some boys might feel excited about the changes happening to their bodies, while others might feel nervous or unsure. Whatever you're feeling, know it's okay, and it's important to talk about your feelings with someone you trust.

Throughout this book, we'll explore all the different aspects of puberty, from physical changes to emotional ups and downs and everything in between. We'll provide you with information, tips, and advice to help you navigate this journey with confidence and understanding. As you continue on this journey, it's important to remember that you're growing not just physically but also mentally and emotionally. Puberty isn't just about the changes you can see on the outside – it's also about the changes happening inside your brain and heart.

Your brain is developing in incredible ways during puberty. You might find that you're able to think more critically, solve problems more easily, and understand complex ideas better than before. This is because your brain is forming new connections and pathways, which is helping you become smarter and more capable every day.

At the same time, you might also notice changes happening in your emotions. You might start to feel more sensitive or moody, or experience sudden bursts of energy or excitement. These changes are perfectly normal and are a sign that your brain is adjusting to all the new experiences and challenges of puberty.

It's important to take care of yourself physically and emotionally during this time. Eating a healthy diet, getting plenty of exercise, and getting enough sleep are all important for your overall well-being. It's also important to take time to relax and do things you enjoy, whether it's playing sports, reading books, or spending time with friends and family.

As you navigate the ups and downs of puberty, remember that it's okay to ask for help if you need it. Whether you're feeling overwhelmed by your emotions or unsure about something happening to your body, plenty of people are here to support you. Talk to your parents, a trusted adult, or a healthcare provider if you have questions or concerns.

Above all, remember to be kind to yourself during this time of change. Puberty can be a rollercoaster ride of emotions and experiences, but it's also an exciting journey full of new discoveries and adventures. Embrace the changes, embrace the growth, and know you are growing into the amazing person you are meant to be. Now that we've discussed the changes happening within you, let's talk about what you can expect in your daily life as you journey through puberty.

One of the first things you might notice is that your daily routine could start to change. As your body grows and develops, you might find that you have different energy levels throughout the day. You might feel more tired in the mornings or find it harder to concentrate in school. This is all normal, and it's a sign that your body is working hard to support all the changes inside you.

You might also find that your interests and hobbies start to shift along with changes in energy levels. You might discover new passions or become more interested in activities you didn't enjoy before. This is because puberty is a time of exploration and self-discovery, and it's natural for your interests to evolve as you grow and change.

In addition to changes in your routine and interests, you might also notice changes happening in your relationships with others. You might feel more independent and want to spend more time with your friends, or you might find that you're more interested in spending time with family members. You might also notice that your relationships with your parents and siblings are evolving as you all navigate the ups and downs of puberty together.

As you continue to grow and change, you might also take on more responsibilities at home and school. You might be expected to help out more with chores around the house or take on leadership roles in group projects at school. While this might feel daunting at times, it's also a sign that you're becoming more mature and capable, and it's an essential part of growing up.

Throughout all these changes, it's important to remember to take care of yourself and prioritize your well-being. Make sure to relax and recharge, and don't be afraid to ask for help if you need it. Whether you're feeling overwhelmed by schoolwork or struggling with your emotions, plenty of people are here to support you every step of the way.

2

HORMONES UNLEASHED: UNDERSTANDING
THE BASICS

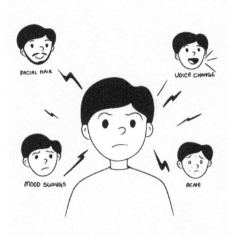

Get ready to dive into the fascinating world of hormones – those tiny, powerful messengers that play a big role in all the changes happening to your body and mind.

Imagine your body as a bustling city, with millions of tiny workers buzzing around, ensuring everything runs smoothly. Well, those tiny workers are your hormones! They're like the busy bees of your body, working tirelessly to keep everything in balance and ensure you grow and develop just how you're supposed to.

But what exactly are hormones, and what do they do? Well, think of them as the directors of your body's orchestra – they control everything from how tall you grow to how your muscles develop to how your emotions fluctuate. They're the reason you're starting to see hair in new places, your voice might be cracking, and you're feeling all those new and exciting emotions.

One of the most important hormones during puberty is called testosterone. You can think of testosterone as the ship's captain – it's responsible for all those classic "boy" changes, like deepening your voice, growing facial hair, and building muscle. But testosterone isn't the only hormone in town – there are plenty of others, like estrogen and progesterone, that play important roles, too, even if they're more commonly associated with girls.

As these hormones surge through your body, they can sometimes make you feel like you're on a wild rollercoaster ride – one minute, you might be feeling on top of the world, and the next, you might feel down in the dumps. But don't worry; this is all a normal part of puberty, and it's a sign that your body is doing exactly what it's supposed to do.

So, as we dive deeper into the world of hormones, get ready to uncover the mysteries of your changing body and mind. Now that we've introduced the concept of hormones, let's take a closer look at some of the specific changes they bring about during puberty.

One of the first signs that hormones are starting to work their magic is the growth spurt. Suddenly, it might seem like you're shooting up like a beanstalk! This rapid growth is fueled by hormones like growth hormone, which stimulate the bones in your body to grow longer and stronger. So don't be surprised if your clothes start feeling a little snug – it's all part of the process!

Along with growing taller, you might also start noticing changes to your body shape. Your shoulders might broaden, your chest might become more defined, and your muscles might start to fill out. This is all thanks to hormones like testosterone, which help build muscle and give you that classic "grown-up" look.

But hormones aren't just responsible for physical changes – they also play a big role in how you feel emotionally. You might find yourself feeling more moody or emotional than usual, or you might experience sudden bursts of energy or excitement. These mood swings are perfectly normal and are a sign that your body is adjusting to all the changes inside you.

In addition to mood swings, hormones can also affect your skin. You might start to notice that your skin becomes oilier or that you're more prone to breakouts and acne. This is because hormones can stimulate the oil glands in your skin to produce more oil, which can clog pores and lead to pimples. But don't worry – there are plenty of ways to keep your skin healthy and clear, like washing your face regularly and avoiding greasy foods.

As you can see, hormones are like the conductors of your body's symphony, orchestrating all the changes that happen during puberty. From physical growth to emotional ups and downs, they play a central role in shaping who you are becoming.

But you must be asking how does that affect me? Well, let me answer you:

One of the most noticeable changes driven by hormones is the development of secondary sexual characteristics. These are the traits that make you look more like an adult. For boys, this might mean growing hair in new places, like on your face, under your arms, and around your genitals. It might also mean that your voice starts to deepen and become more resonant, thanks to the growth of your vocal cords.

Additionally, hormones like testosterone are responsible for the growth of your testicles and penis. You might notice that your testicles start to get larger and that your penis grows in size. This is all perfectly normal and is part of the process of becoming a grown-up man.

Another important change driven by hormones is the development of sexual feelings and desires. You might start to notice that you're attracted to people in a different way than you were before. You might find yourself thinking about kissing, dating, or even having sex. These feelings are all a natural part of growing up, and they're nothing to be ashamed of. Just remember to always treat yourself and others with respect and kindness.

Hormones can also have an impact on your mood and emotions during puberty. You might find that you're more irritable or moody than usual or that you're experiencing more intense emotions, like sadness or anger. This is all completely normal and is a sign that your body is adjusting to all the changes happening inside of you. Remember to be patient with yourself and to reach out for support if you need it.

As you can see, hormones are incredibly powerful chemicals that play a central role in shaping who you are becoming during puberty. From physical changes like growing hair and deepening your voice to emotional changes like developing sexual feelings and experiencing mood swings, they're responsible for a wide range of transformations in your body and mind.

So, as you continue on this journey of puberty, remember to embrace each new change with curiosity and courage. With patience, perseverance, and a positive attitude, you'll navigate the world of hormones like a seasoned explorer, emerging stronger, wiser, and more confident than ever before.

Firstly, it's important to remember that everyone experiences puberty differently. Some boys might start noticing changes earlier or later than others, and that's completely normal. Don't compare yourself to your friends or classmates – focus on your own journey and trust that your body knows what it's doing.

Secondly, communication is key. Talk to your parents, guardians, or another trusted adult about what you're experiencing. They've been through puberty themselves and can offer guidance and support. If you're feeling uncomfortable or confused about any changes, don't be afraid to ask questions – no question is silly when it comes to understanding your body.

Additionally, educate yourself about puberty. Books like this, reliable websites, and even your school's health education classes can provide valuable information about what to expect during puberty and how to take care of yourself. Knowledge is power; the more you understand what's happening to your body, the more confident you'll feel about navigating these changes.

Next, take care of your physical health. Eat a balanced diet, get regular exercise, and prioritize sleep. Taking care of your body will help you feel better physically and improve your mood and overall well-being during this time of change.

Lastly, be kind to yourself. Puberty can be a rollercoaster of emotions, and it's normal to feel overwhelmed or uncertain at times. Remember that it's okay to ask for help if needed, and don't be too hard on yourself if things feel challenging. You're growing and changing in so many ways, and that's something to be celebrated!

3

THE MYSTERIOUS WORLD OF FACIAL HAIR

Have you ever seen your dad sporting a mustache worthy of a pirate captain? Ever wonder why some older dudes have beards that tickle your face when they hug? Then prepare to dive headfirst into the wild, wooly world of facial hair! This ain't no boring biology lesson, though. Think secret codes, superhero disguises, and epic battles between razor and fuzz. Let's be honest: some dudes out there look like they glued cotton balls to their chin, but others rock beards that would make even Santa jealous. So, buckle up, young adventurers, because you're about to embark on a journey to decode the mysteries of whiskers, stubble, and everything in between.

Forget boring old textbooks; picture this: imagine yourself as a fearless explorer venturing into uncharted territory, your flashlight (curiosity) in hand. This uncharted territory, my friends, is your own face! You'll be charting the first signs of fuzz, mapping out potential mustache territories, and deciphering the secret language of beard styles. Is a goatee a sign of wisdom or mischief? Does a handlebar mustache whisper tales of adventure or silliness? These are the questions, brave explorers, that this book will help you answer!

Think of growing up as a grand adventure, complete with milestones and challenges. One of those challenges, you guessed it, is facial hair. It's like a superpower that gradually unlocks as you get older. But with great power comes great responsibility (don't worry, it's not as heavy as it sounds!). This book will be your trusty guide, teaching you everything you need to know about caring for your future facial forest, from the proper way to tame a stray whisker to the coolest styles to try (when the time comes, of course!).

So, are you ready to embark on this hairy quest? Are you prepared to become a master of mustache knowledge, a beard whisperer, or a champion of chin fluff? If your answer is a resounding "Heck yeah!", then flip the page and let the adventure begin! Remember, growing up is full of surprises, and facial hair is just one of the many exciting chapters waiting to be written. Let's explore it together, shall we?

Facial hair, often seen as a symbol of maturity and masculinity, is one of boys' most visible signs of puberty. It typically begins to appear around the ages of 12 to 16, although the timing can vary widely from person to person. You might notice fine hairs sprouting on your upper lip, chin, cheeks, and neck. These hairs might be light and wispy initially, but with time and patience, they'll grow thicker and more noticeable.

But what exactly causes facial hair to grow? The answer lies in the magical world of hormones, particularly testosterone. As your body produces more testosterone during puberty, it stimulates the hair follicles on your face to grow thicker and coarser hairs. This process can take months or even years to develop fully, so don't be discouraged if your facial hair doesn't appear right away – it's all part of the journey.

As your facial hair grows, you might feel excited, proud, and maybe even a little self-conscious. It's perfectly normal to have mixed emotions about this new milestone. Some boys embrace their facial hair as a sign of maturity and embrace the opportunity to experiment with different styles, while others might feel unsure or anxious about their changing appearance.

If you're feeling unsure about how to manage your facial hair, don't worry – you're not alone. Many boys navigate this new territory with a combination of trial and error, experimentation, and guidance from others. Here are a few tips to help you navigate the mysterious world of facial hair:

Patience is key:

Facial hair growth takes time, so be patient and allow your beard or mustache to grow at its own pace. Don't be discouraged if it seems slow at first – with time and persistence, you'll achieve the desired look.

Experiment with styles:

Once your facial hair starts to grow, have fun experimenting with different styles and shapes. Whether you prefer a clean-shaven look, a rugged stubble, or a full beard, there's no right or wrong way to rock your facial hair.

Practice good grooming habits:

Regular grooming is essential for keeping your facial hair looking its best. Invest in a quality razor, trimmer, or grooming kit, and establish a routine for shaving, trimming, and maintaining your beard or mustache.

Seek guidance:

If you're feeling overwhelmed or uncertain about how to care for your facial hair, don't hesitate to seek guidance from a trusted adult, barber, or online resources. They can offer advice, tips, and techniques to help you achieve the look you desire.

Remember, facial hair is a natural and normal part of growing up, and there's no one-size-fits-all approach to grooming or styling. Embrace your unique journey, celebrate your newfound whiskers, and wear them proudly. Whether you're rocking a full beard or stylish stubble, your facial hair reflects your individuality and masculinity. So go forth, brave adventurers, and explore the mysterious world of facial hair with confidence and flair.

As you embark on your journey through the mysterious world of facial hair, there are a few more things to remember to ensure you navigate this terrain confidently and in style.

Maintain hygiene:

Just like the hair on your head, your facial hair requires regular washing to keep it clean and healthy. Use a gentle cleanser or shampoo to wash your beard or mustache regularly, and be sure to rinse thoroughly to remove any product buildup or debris.

Moisturize:

Facial hair can sometimes be dry and itchy, especially as it grows longer. Consider using a beard oil or balm to keep your skin and beard moisturized. These products help hydrate your skin and soften your facial hair, making it more manageable and comfortable to groom.

Trim with care:

Trimming is essential to maintaining your facial hair, but it's important to do so with care. Invest in a quality pair of scissors or a beard trimmer, and take your time to trim your beard or mustache evenly and symmetrically. Start with a longer setting and gradually trim down until you achieve your desired length.

Embrace imperfections:

Not every patch of facial hair will grow in perfectly, and that's okay! Embrace the unique quirks and characteristics of your beard or mustache, and don't get discouraged by any sparse areas or uneven growth. Your facial hair will continue to fill in and develop with time and patience.

Be confident:

Above all, remember to be confident in your appearance and embrace the journey of growing facial hair. Whether you're sporting a full beard, a stylish goatee, or a simple stubble, wear your facial hair with pride and confidence. Your beard or mustache reflects your individuality and masculinity, so own it with confidence and swagger.

As you continue to explore the mysterious world of facial hair, remember that your journey is unique and personal. Embrace the changes, celebrate your newfound whiskers, and have fun experimenting with different styles and looks. Whether you're a seasoned beard enthusiast or just starting to grow your first few hairs, the world of facial hair is full of endless possibilities and adventures. So go forth, fearless adventurers, and conquer the world – one whisker at a time!

4

VOICE EVOLUTION: FROM SQUEAKS TO BOOMS

Yo, vocal wizards! Ever wondered why your voice cracks like a haunted pirate ship one minute, then sounds smoother than a jazz singer the next? Buckle up because we're about to embark on a mind-blowing journey through the mysterious world of... your voice!

Forget boring lectures about vocal cords and stuff (although that's pretty cool too). This is about the real magic: how your voice transforms from squeaky giggles to booming pronouncements, all while navigating the hilarious chaos of puberty. Think of it as a superpower that activates as you grow, and let me tell you, this ain't just about hitting high notes (or, well, maybe it is sometimes!).

Imagine yourself as a vocal explorer, venturing into the uncharted territory of your own throat. You'll decipher the code of squeaks, cracks, and booming pronouncements, mapping out the path from chipmunk cheeks to superhero baritone. Is a raspy voice a sign of coolness or mystery? Does a high-pitched squeal indicate excitement or fear? These are the questions, young Padawans of the vocal arts, that this book will help you answer!

Imagine growing up as an epic adventure, and your voice is the soundtrack. It's the battle cry of the playground, the secret whisper shared with friends, the laugh that can erupt like a volcano. But with great vocal power comes great responsibility (don't worry, it's way more fun than it sounds!). This book will be your trusty guide, teaching you how to confidently use your voice, from mastering those tricky pitch changes to belting out your favorite tunes without fear.

So, are you ready to unleash your inner vocal beast? Are you prepared to become a master of the squeak-to-boom, a whisperer of words, a champion of vocal variety? Remember, your voice is your unique instrument, and growing up is all about learning to play it like a rockstar. Let's explore its potential together, shall we?

As you journey through puberty, you may notice that your voice transforms remarkably. Gone are the days of high-pitched squeaks and giggles – instead, you'll find yourself blessed with a deeper, more resonant voice that commands attention and respect.

But how does this magical transformation occur? The answer lies within your vocal cords, a pair of elastic bands located in your larynx, or voice box. During puberty, your body produces hormones like testosterone, which stimulates the growth and thickening of your vocal cords. This causes your vocal cords to lengthen and become denser, resulting in a lower-pitched voice.

The process of voice evolution typically begins around the ages of 12 to 16 for boys, although the timing can vary from person to person. You might notice that your voice starts to crack or break as it transitions from its higher childhood pitch to its lower adult pitch. This can be an exciting – and sometimes embarrassing – experience, but rest assured that it's a perfectly normal part of growing up.

As your voice continues to deepen, you'll likely notice other changes as well. Your speech patterns might change, with your words sounding more mature and authoritative. You might also find that you can project your voice more confidently and effectively, whether speaking in front of a crowd or simply conversing with friends.

Embracing your evolving voice can be an empowering experience, but it's important to remember that everyone's voice evolves at its own pace. Some boys might experience a sudden and dramatic drop in pitch, while others might notice more gradual changes over time. Whatever the case may be, know that your voice is unique and special, and it reflects who you are as a person.

Remember that you're not alone if you're feeling self-conscious or unsure about your changing voice. Many boys navigate this journey with a combination of excitement and apprehension, and it's perfectly normal to have mixed emotions about it. Talk to your parents, guardians, or another trusted adult about your feelings, and don't hesitate to seek guidance or support if you need it.

As you continue through voice evolution, there are a few more aspects to consider to help you navigate this exciting and sometimes challenging terrain.

Practice speaking:

Embrace opportunities to practice using your evolving voice. Whether it's reading aloud, participating in class discussions, or engaging in conversations with friends and family, regular practice can help you feel more confident and comfortable with your changing voice.

Stay hydrated:

Keeping your vocal cords hydrated is essential for maintaining a healthy and vibrant voice. Drink plenty of water throughout the day to ensure that your vocal cords stay lubricated and flexible. Avoid excessive caffeine and alcohol, as they can cause dehydration and irritate your throat.

Warm up your voice:

Just like athletes warm up their muscles before a workout, it's important to warm up your voice extensively before speaking or singing. Simple vocal warm-up exercises, such as humming, lip trills, and gentle sirens, can help prepare your vocal cords for optimal performance and reduce the risk of strain or injury.

Listen to your body:

Pay attention to how your voice feels and sounds, and listen to your body's cues. If you experience hoarseness, fatigue, or discomfort while speaking, take a break and rest your voice.

Overworking your vocal cords can lead to strain and damage, so listening to your body and practicing self-care is important.

Seek professional guidance:

If you're interested in developing your voice further, consider seeking guidance from a vocal coach or speech therapist. These professionals can provide personalized instruction and exercises to help you strengthen and improve your voice, whether you're interested in singing, public speaking, or simply enhancing your communication skills.

Embrace your unique voice:

Your voice reflects your individuality and personality, so embrace its unique qualities and characteristics. Whether you have a deep, booming voice or a lighter, more melodic tone, celebrate the beauty and diversity of your voice and use it to express yourself authentically and confidently.

Embrace the opportunity to explore and celebrate your evolving voice, and remember to practice self-care and listen to your body along the way. With patience, practice, and a positive attitude, you'll navigate the journey of voice evolution with confidence and grace, emerging with a strong, expressive, and unique voice.

Did you know your nose affects your voice? Try pinching your nose and speaking - sounds different, right?

Singers warm up their voices just like athletes warm up their muscles. What exercises could you do to "warm up" your voice?

Your voice is like a fingerprint - no two are exactly alike! How would you describe your own voice?

Time for some more facts:

Age Range	Voice Changes	What's Happening?	Fun Facts
0-2 years	Gurgles, coos, laughs, cries	Learning basic communication through sounds	Can recognize parents' voices by three months
2-4 years	Babbling, simple words, first questions	Vocal cords strengthening, exploring different sounds	"Mama" is the most spoken word worldwide
4-6 years	Sentences, increasing articulation, singing begins	Brain-voice connection developing, expressing emotions	Children learn languages faster than adults
6-8 years	More complex sentences, clearer pronunciation	Voice control improves, starting to sound more "grown-up"	Boys' voices start to deepen slightly
8-10 years	Pitch fluctuations, occasional cracks	Puberty's effects begin, vocal cords changing rapidly	This is where things get interesting (and sometimes embarrassing!)
10-13 years	Voice cracks become frequent, wider pitch range	Major growth spurt in vocal cords, leading to unpredictable changes	Girls' voices also deepen, but not as dramatically
13+	Voice stabilizes, individual tone develops	Vocal cords reach adult size, uniqueness emerges	You've officially "found your voice"!

This is a general timeline, and individual experiences will vary. And a reminder that it is all perfectly normal...

Plus, your voice is more than just a tool for communication – it's a powerful instrument that reflects your identity, emotions, and personality. Here are a few more tips to help you embrace and celebrate your evolving voice:

Express yourself:

Your voice is a powerful tool for self-expression, so don't be afraid to let it be heard. Whether you're speaking up for what you believe in, sharing your thoughts and ideas, or expressing your emotions through song or spoken word, let your voice reflect who you are and what you stand for.

Practice active listening:

Listening is an important part of effective communication, so try to actively listen to others when they speak. Pay attention to the tone, pitch, and inflection of their voices and the underlying emotions and messages they convey. By practicing active listening, you'll strengthen your communication skills and deepen your connections with others.

Use your voice for good:

Your voice can inspire, uplift, and empower others, so use it wisely and responsibly. Whether you're speaking out against injustice, advocating for positive change, or simply offering words of encouragement to those in need, your voice can make a difference in the world around you. So, speak up for what you believe in and use your voice as a force for good.

Embrace vocal diversity:

Just as every person is unique, so too is every voice. Embrace the diversity of voices in the world around you and celebrate the richness and variety of human expression. Whether you're drawn to deep, resonant voices or light, melodious tones, appreciate the beauty and complexity of vocal diversity and use it as inspiration for your own voice journey.

Be patient and persistent:

Voice evolution is a gradual process that takes time and patience, so be kind to yourself and trust in your body's natural abilities. Celebrate your progress so far, and continue to nurture and develop your voice with persistence and dedication. With time and practice, you'll continue to grow and evolve as a vocal artist and communicator.

Embrace the opportunity to explore and celebrate your evolving voice, and remember to use it as a tool for self-expression, connection, and positive change. With patience, practice, and a spirit of adventure, you'll navigate the journey of voice evolution with confidence and grace, emerging with a voice that is strong, expressive, and uniquely yours. So, raise your voice high and proud, fearless adventurers, and let the world hear the magnificent sound of your evolution!

5

THE LOWDOWN ON ADAM'S APPLE

Dude, What's That Bump on Your Throat?

Ever notice a weird bump popping up on your neck, right about where your superhero cape would start? Feeling a little self-conscious about it? Don't worry, you're not alone! That strange bump is called an Adam's apple, and let me tell you, it's got a story wilder than your wildest adventure comic.

Forget boring lectures about anatomy (although, hey, the human body is pretty cool too). This is about cracking the code of your body, like a detective on a mission! We'll unravel the mystery of the Adam's apple, from its surprising origins to its secret superpowers (yes, you read that right!).

Imagine yourself as a body explorer, venturing into the uncharted territory of your own neck. You'll be deciphering the clues of muscles, bones, and cartilage, piecing together the puzzle of why that bump decided to show up. Is it a sign of growing up, an alien communication device, or maybe a secret weapon for epic burping contests? These are the questions, young Padawans of self-discovery, that this chapter will help you answer!

Imagine growing up as an epic quest, and your body is the map. It's full of hidden secrets and exciting changes, and the Adam's apple is just one stop on the adventure. But with great bodily mysteries come great questions (don't worry, they're the fun kind!). This chapter will be your trusty guide, teaching you everything you ever wanted to know about your Adam's apple, from its hilarious nickname to its role in that cool, deep voice you're starting to develop.

So, are you ready to unlock the secrets of your very own body? Are you prepared to become a master of the Adam's apple knowledge, a whisperer of anatomy, a champion of self-discovery? Remember, your body is amazing, and growing up is all about learning to appreciate its awesomeness. Let's explore it together, shall we?

What exactly is this curious bump on your throat, and why does it seem to appear out of nowhere during puberty?

Well, my young adventurer, Adam's apple – also known as the laryngeal prominence – is actually part of your voice box or larynx. It's made up of cartilage, the same stuff that makes your ears and nose flexible, and it sits right on top of your windpipe or trachea. But why does it stick out more prominently in boys than in girls? Ah, that's where the plot thickens!

During puberty, your body goes through some pretty radical changes thanks to hormones like testosterone. And one of those changes involves the growth of your Adam's apple. As your vocal cords lengthen and your larynx grows larger, the cartilage that forms the Adam's apple becomes more pronounced, giving you that classic "Adam's apple" bump on your throat.

But here's the real kicker – the Adam's apple isn't just for show. It actually serves a pretty important purpose in your body's grand design. You see, the Adam's apple helps protect your vocal cords and regulate the pitch of your voice. When you speak or sing, your vocal cords vibrate against each other, producing sound. The Adam's apple helps control the tension and length of your vocal cords, allowing you to produce different pitches and tones with your voice.

So, far from being just a strange bump on your throat, Adam's apple is actually a key player in the symphony of your voice. It's a symbol of your journey through puberty and a reminder of the incredible changes happening inside your body.

But wait, there's more! Did you know the Adam's apple has a few other tricks up its sleeve? That's right – it's not just for regulating your voice. In some cultures, the size of a man's Adam's apple is thought to be a sign of masculinity and strength. In folklore, Adam's apple has been associated with forbidden knowledge and temptation, thanks to its connection to the biblical story of Adam and Eve.

But the story of the Adam's apple story doesn't end there, oh no! This seemingly innocuous bump has also captured the imagination of artists, writers, and thinkers throughout history. From ancient myths and legends to modern-day literature and art, the Adam's apple has fascinated and inspired countless generations.

In literature, the Adam's apple has been used to symbolize temptation, desire, and the quest for knowledge. In Nathaniel Hawthorne's classic novel "The Scarlet Letter," the character of Hester Prynne is described as having a "small, dark, and nearly imperceptible" Adam's apple, symbolizing her defiance of societal norms and her pursuit of truth and freedom.

The Adam's apple has been depicted in countless paintings, sculptures, and illustrations, often as a symbol of masculinity, strength, and vitality. In Leonardo da Vinci's famous drawing "Vitruvian Man," the Adam's apple is prominently featured, emphasizing the connection between the human body and the natural world.

But perhaps the most enduring legacy of the Adam's apple is its role in popular culture and folklore. In movies, television shows, and comic books, Adam's apple has been used as a visual shorthand for masculinity and toughness, often appearing on rugged heroes and daring adventurers. In folklore and mythology, the Adam's apple has been associated with wisdom, forbidden knowledge, and the mysteries of the universe.

So, the next time you feel self-conscious about that bump on your throat, remember that you're not just carrying around a piece of cartilage – you're carrying around a piece of history, a symbol of humanity's endless quest for understanding and self-discovery. Embrace, celebrate, and wear it with pride, my young adventurer. Your Adam's apple is a badge of honor, a testament to your growth and transformation, and a reminder of life's incredible journey.

And who knows? Maybe one day, you'll uncover even more secrets within your own body's depths. Until then, keep exploring, learning, and marveling at the wonders of the human form. Adventure awaits, my friend – so go forth and conquer the world, Adam's apple and all!

6

GROWING UP: NAVIGATING HEIGHT SPURTS

Have you ever woken up one morning feeling like your bed shrunk overnight? Suddenly, find your favorite jeans looking like capris. Brace yourself, young adventurer, because you're about to embark on a thrilling rollercoaster ride called... puberty! And one of the wildest twists and turns on this journey is the infamous height spurt!

Forget boring charts and graphs (although seeing how you stack up can be pretty cool too). This is about understanding the amazing transformations inside your body like a superhero unlocking hidden powers! We will explore the science behind those sudden growth spurts, from bone-building battles to the secrets of those creaky knees.

Imagine yourself as a growth explorer, venturing into the uncharted territory of your own skeleton. You'll decipher the code of muscles, bones, and hormones, figuring out why you're suddenly towering over your little sister (or vice versa!). Is it magic? Superfood smoothies? Nope, it's the incredible process of growing up!

Imagine growing up as an epic adventure; your body is the ultimate transformer. It's constantly changing, adapting, and surprising you with new abilities. Height spurts are just one chapter in this exciting story, but with great growing power comes some hilarious challenges (don't worry, they're also totally relatable!). This chapter will be your trusty guide, teaching you everything you need to know about navigating those sudden growth spurts, from finding pants that fit to rocking your new giraffe-like grace.

So, are you ready to embrace the ups and downs (literally!) of height spurts? Are you prepared to become a master of growing knowledge, a whisperer of bones, a champion of body positivity? Remember, growing up is a unique journey for everyone, and this chapter is here to help you navigate it with laughter, understanding, and maybe even a little extra duct tape for those pants that are too short. Let's explore it together, shall we?

Now, we're tackling a topic that's close to every growing boy's heart – height spurts. Strap yourselves in as we embark on a rollercoaster ride through the ups and downs of growing taller and discover how to navigate this wild ride with style and grace.

Picture this: one day, you're cruising along, feeling perfectly comfortable in your own skin, and the next – bam! – you wake up to find that your pants are suddenly too short, your sleeves are too tight, and you're looking everyone in the eye instead of up at them. Sound familiar? Congratulations, my friend – you're amidst a height spurt!

Height spurts, also known as growth spurts, are a perfectly normal and natural part of growing up. During puberty, your body undergoes rapid growth and development, fueled by hormones like growth hormone and testosterone. This can cause you to shoot up like a beanstalk practically overnight, leaving you feeling like you're living in a world of giants.

But fear not brave adventurer – there are plenty of ways to navigate the ups and downs of height spurts confidently and easily. Here are a few tips to help weather the storm:

Embrace the changes:

Growing taller can be an exciting and sometimes intimidating experience. Embrace the changes happening to your body and celebrate your newfound height with pride. Remember, growing taller is a sign of health and vitality, and it's nothing to be ashamed of.

Update your wardrobe:

As you grow taller, your clothing may start to feel snug or uncomfortable. Take this opportunity to update your wardrobe with clothes that fit your changing body. Invest in pants with adjustable waistbands, extra-length shirts, and shoes with plenty of room for your growing feet.

Practice good posture:

As your body adjusts to its new height, you may experience changes in your posture and balance. Practice good posture by standing up straight, keeping your shoulders back, and distributing your weight evenly between your feet. Not only will this help you look taller and more confident, but it will also support your spine and prevent back pain.

Eat a healthy diet:

A balanced diet rich in nutrients like protein, calcium, and vitamins is essential for supporting healthy growth and development during puberty. Ensure you include plenty of fruits, vegetables, whole grains, and lean proteins in your meals, and limit sugary snacks and processed foods. Drinking plenty of water is also important for staying hydrated and supporting cellular growth.

Get plenty of sleep:

Adequate sleep is crucial for supporting growth and development during puberty. Aim for 8-10 hours of sleep per night to give your body the rest it needs to grow and repair itself. Establishing a consistent bedtime routine and creating a relaxing sleep environment can help you get the quality sleep your body craves.

Stay active:

Regular exercise is essential for supporting healthy growth and development and maintaining strong muscles and bones. Engage in a variety of physical activities that you enjoy, such as sports, swimming, biking, or dancing. Aim for at least 60 minutes of moderate to vigorous activity daily to keep your body strong and fit.

By embracing the changes, updating your wardrobe, practicing good posture, eating a healthy diet, getting plenty of sleep, and staying active, you can navigate the ups and downs of height spurts with confidence and ease.

Remember that everyone grows at their own pace, and height spurts can vary in duration and intensity from person to person. Be patient with yourself and trust that your body knows what it's doing. Even if you feel like you're towering over your friends one day and lagging behind the next, know that it's all part of the natural growth rhythm.

Embrace your uniqueness:

Your height is just one aspect of who you are, and it doesn't define your worth or value as a person. Embrace your unique qualities and celebrate the things that make you special – your sense of humor, creativity, or kindness towards others. Remember that true greatness comes from within and has nothing to do with how tall you are.

Seek support:

If you're feeling overwhelmed or unsure about the changes happening to your body, don't be afraid to reach out for support. Talk to your parents, guardians, or another trusted adult about your feelings, and don't hesitate to ask questions or express your concerns. You're not alone on this journey, and plenty of people care about you and want to help you navigate the challenges of growing taller.

Enjoy the ride:

Growing taller is an exciting – albeit sometimes awkward – adventure, so don't forget to enjoy the journey! Embrace the opportunities that come with your newfound height, whether it's reaching the top shelf without a step stool or finally being tall enough to ride the roller coaster at the amusement park. Life is full of ups and downs, twists and turns, and growing taller is just one of many exhilarating experiences along the way.

Height spurts are a normal and natural part of growing up, and they're nothing to be afraid of. By embracing the changes, staying active, eating a healthy diet, getting plenty of sleep, and seeking support when you need it, you can navigate the ups and downs of growing taller with confidence and grace. Remember to be patient with yourself, embrace your uniqueness, and enjoy the ride – because before you know it, you'll be standing tall and proud, ready to take on whatever adventures come your way. So, here's to growing up, my fellow adventurers – may your height spurts be swift, your adventures be thrilling, and your journey be filled with joy and discovery!

7

PIMPLES AND MORE: THE SKIN SAGA

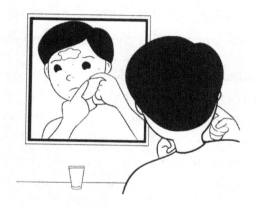

Pimples, Patches, and Poppin' Questions...

Ever wake up looking like a pepperoni pizza, complete with extra red dots? Feeling like your face is waging a secret war against itself, with patches and flakes taking center stage? Don't despair, brave adventurer, because you're not alone! Welcome to the Skin Saga, a wild and sometimes wacky chapter in the grand adventure of growing up.

Forget boring lectures about pores and sebum (although understanding your skin is pretty cool, too!). This is about conquering the mysteries of your own face, like a detective on a mission to solve the case of the mystery pimple. We're going to crack the code of your skin, from figuring out why it acts up to discovering ninja-level skincare moves. Is it aliens? Bad pizza? Nope, it's just your body saying, "Hey, I'm changing!"

Imagine yourself as a skin explorer, venturing into the uncharted territory of your own face. You'll decipher the clues of oil glands, hormones, and bacteria, piecing together the puzzle of why your skin sometimes throws a tantrum. Can you befriend the good bacteria? Outsmart the oil slicks? These are the questions, young Padawans of self-care, that this chapter will help you answer!

Imagine growing up as an epic quest, and your skin is the battleground. It's full of unexpected twists and turns, victories, and occasional meltdowns, but that's all part of the adventure! With great skin-care power comes great responsibility (don't worry, it's more about learning than bossing your face around!). This chapter will be your trusty guide, teaching you everything you ever wanted to know about your skin, from the science behind those pesky pimples to the secrets of a healthy glow.

So, are you ready to unlock the secrets of your skin and become a master of its mysteries? Are you prepared to become a pimple-defeating warrior, a hydration hero, or a self-confidence champion? Remember, your skin is unique and amazing, and this chapter is here to help you navigate its ups and downs with knowledge, humor, and maybe a little bit of laughter (because, let's face it, some skin days are just funny!).

Fear not, brave adventurers – you're not alone in this skin saga. Pimples are a common – albeit annoying – part of puberty, thanks to changes in hormone levels that can lead to increased oil production and clogged pores. While it may feel like pimples are taking over your face, rest assured that they're a temporary inconvenience and can be managed with the right care and attention.

So, how do you navigate the treacherous waters of pimple-prone skin? Fear not, for I have assembled a trusty arsenal of tips and tricks to help you conquer the skin saga once and for all:

Practice good skincare:

Keeping your skin clean is essential for preventing pimples and maintaining a healthy complexion. Wash your face twice a day with a gentle cleanser and remove any makeup or sunscreen before bedtime. Avoid harsh scrubbing or overwashing, which can irritate your skin and worsen acne.

Use non-comedogenic products:

Opt for non-comedogenic formulas that won't clog your pores when choosing skincare products. Look for labels that say "oil-free" or "non-comedogenic," and avoid heavy creams or lotions that may exacerbate acne. Stick to lightweight, water-based products that won't weigh down your skin.

Avoid touching your face:

As tempting as it may be, avoid touching or picking at your pimples. This can spread bacteria and lead to further inflammation and scarring. Instead, keep your hands away from your face and resist the urge to squeeze or pop your pimples.

Manage stress:

Stress can exacerbate acne, so finding healthy ways to manage stress and relax is important. Practice relaxation techniques such as deep breathing, meditation, or yoga, and make time for activities that bring you joy and peace of mind.

Eat a healthy diet:

While diet alone won't cure acne, eating a balanced diet rich in fruits, vegetables, whole grains, and lean proteins can support overall skin health. Limit sugary snacks, processed foods, and greasy foods, which can contribute to acne flare-ups.

Stay hydrated:

Drinking plenty of water is essential for keeping your skin hydrated and healthy. Aim for at least eight glasses of water daily, and avoid excessive caffeine or sugary drinks, which can dehydrate your skin.

Seek professional help if needed:

If you're struggling to manage your acne on your own, don't hesitate to seek help from a dermatologist. They can offer personalized treatment options, such as prescription medications or topical treatments, to help you get your acne under control.

It's crucial to understand that dealing with pimples and other skin changes during puberty is completely normal. You're not alone in this journey – nearly every teenager experiences some form of acne or skin blemishes at some point during puberty. It's just one of the many exciting – albeit sometimes frustrating – changes that come with growing up.

During puberty, hormonal fluctuations can increase oil production in the skin, which can clog pores and result in pimples, blackheads, and whiteheads. While it may feel like your skin is rebelling against you, rest assured that these changes are temporary and often improve with time and proper care.

It's important to remember that having pimples or acne doesn't mean there's anything wrong with you or your skin. Acne is not a reflection of your cleanliness or personal hygiene – it's a natural part of puberty. So, don't be too hard on yourself if you're dealing with a breakout – it happens to the best of us!

You can navigate the skin saga with confidence and grace by practicing good skincare habits, managing stress, eating a healthy diet, staying hydrated, and seeking professional help if needed. Remember to be patient with yourself and your skin, and don't hesitate to reach out for support if you're struggling.

As you journey through the skin saga, remember that the condition of your skin does not determine your worth and value as a person. You are so much more than the bumps and blemishes that may appear on your face. Your true beauty lies in your kindness, compassion, and inner strength.

It's also important to recognize that everyone's skin is unique, and what works for one person may not work for another. So, don't get discouraged if you try different skincare products or treatments and don't see immediate results. Finding the right skincare routine takes time and experimentation, so be patient and keep trying until you find what works best for you.

And remember, you are not alone on this journey. If you're feeling overwhelmed or unsure about how to care for your skin, don't hesitate to ask for help. Talk to your parents, guardians, or a trusted adult about your concerns, and consider seeking guidance from a dermatologist or skincare professional. They can offer personalized advice and treatment options to help you achieve clear, healthy skin.

Above all, remember to be kind to yourself. Puberty can be challenging, filled with ups and downs, twists and turns. But through it all, remember that you are strong, resilient, and capable of overcoming any obstacle that comes your way. Embrace the journey, embrace your skin, and know that you are enough, just as you are.

8

THE DEBUT OF THE DEEPENING VOICE

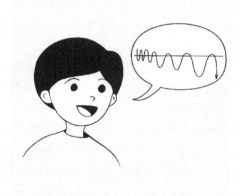

Are you ready for a sound revolution? Remember those high-pitched squeaks that could shatter glass? Well, buckle up because they're about to be replaced by... booming pronouncements, smooth whispers, and maybe even the occasional embarrassing crackle! It's time to dive into the wild world of your changing voice, a thrilling chapter in the grand adventure of growing up.

Forget boring biology lessons about vocal cords and stuff (although that's pretty cool, too!). This is about understanding the incredible transformation happening right inside your throat, like a superhero discovering a hidden power! We'll explore the science behind the deepening voice, from the rumble of hormones to the secrets of those mysterious cracks. Is it magic? Superfood smoothies? Nope, it's the amazing process of puberty!

Imagine yourself as a vocal explorer, venturing into the uncharted territory of your own larynx. You'll decipher the code of muscles, cartilage, and hormones, figuring out why your voice suddenly sounds like a record player at slow speed. Is it a sign of coolness? Superpowers in the making? These are the questions, young Padawans of vocal evolution, that this chapter will help you answer!

Imagine growing up in an epic quest, and your voice is the soundtrack. It's the battle cry on the playground, the secret whisper shared with friends, the laugh that can erupt like a volcano. But with great vocal power comes great responsibility (don't worry, it's way more fun than it sounds!). This chapter will be your trusty guide, teaching you everything you need to know about navigating your voice's exciting (and sometimes hilarious) changes. From mastering those tricky pitch changes to belting out your favorite tunes without fear, you'll learn how to use your voice with confidence and style.

So, are you ready to unleash your inner vocal beast? Are you prepared to become a master of the crackle-to-boom, a whisperer of words, a champion of vocal variety? Remember, your voice is your unique instrument, and growing up is all about learning to play it like a rockstar.

Your deepening voice is a powerful and exciting development, signaling your transition from boyhood to manhood. As your vocal cords lengthen and thicken, thanks to hormones like testosterone, your voice will gradually become deeper, richer, and more resonant. It's a sign of maturity and growth and something to be celebrated!

However, getting used to your new voice can be a journey in itself. You may experiment with different pitches and tones, trying to find your voice in this brave new world. You may also experience moments of self-consciousness or insecurity as you adjust to the changes happening to your voice. But fear not – with time, patience, and a bit of practice, you'll learn to embrace and master your deepening voice like a seasoned pro.

So, how can you navigate the debut of the deepening voice with confidence and grace? Fear not, for I have assembled a trusty guide to help you on your journey:

Embrace the changes:

Your deepening voice is a natural and exciting part of growing up, so embrace it with pride! Celebrate your voice's newfound richness and depth, and don't be afraid to let it be heard.

Practice speaking:

As your voice continues to deepen, you may adjust your speech patterns and vocal inflections. Practice speaking in different tones and pitches, and experiment with projecting your voice confidently and effectively.

Be patient:

Adjusting to your new voice may take time, so be patient with yourself as you navigate this exciting – and sometimes awkward – transition. Remember, Rome wasn't built in a day, and neither is a masterful speaking voice!

Seek feedback:

If you're unsure about how your voice sounds or how others perceive it, don't hesitate to seek feedback from friends, family, or a trusted mentor. Constructive feedback can help you refine your vocal skills and build confidence in your speaking abilities.

Embrace vocal diversity:

Just as every person is unique, so is every voice. Embrace the diversity of voices in the world around you and celebrate the beauty and complexity of vocal expression.

Remember, your voice is a powerful communication, self-expression, and connection tool. Whether you're delivering a speech, singing a song, or engaging in conversation with friends, let your voice reflect your confidence, authenticity, and inner strength.

Your voice is evolving just like the rest of your body, and it's something to be celebrated! Embrace the changes with pride, and don't be afraid to let your new voice be heard. Practice speaking in different tones and pitches, and experiment with projecting your voice confidently and effectively. Be patient with yourself as you adjust to your new vocal abilities – mastering your deepening voice takes time and practice. Seek feedback from friends, family, or a trusted mentor to help refine your vocal skills and build confidence in your speaking abilities.

Your voice is the most powerful tool for communication, self-expression, and connection. Let it reflect your confidence, authenticity, and inner strength as you continue on your journey through puberty. With time, practice, and a dash of courage, you'll master the art of the deepening voice and emerge as a confident, powerful communicator.

So, my fellow adventurers, as you continue on your quest through puberty, remember that your deepening voice is a badge of honor, a symbol of your growth and transformation. Embrace, celebrate, and let it be heard loud and proud! With time, practice, and a dash of courage, you'll master the art of the deepening voice and emerge as a confident, powerful communicator. So, raise your voice high, my friends, and let the world hear the magnificent sound of your evolution!

9

BOXER BRIEFS OR BRIEFS: DECODING UNDERWEAR CHOICES

Undy Decisions.

Do you ever stare at your underwear drawer, feeling more lost than a penguin in the Sahara? Are you torn between the freedom of boxers and the snugness of briefs? Well, hold onto your socks, young adventurer, because you're about to embark on a thrilling quest: The Great Underpants Adventure! We're diving deep into the world of underwear choices, unraveling the mysteries of boxers, briefs, and everything in between.

Forget boring lectures about fabrics and stitching (although comfort matters!). This is about conquering the complexities of your own nether regions like a detective trying to find the perfect under-suit sidekick. We're going to crack the code of comfort, style, and practicality, figuring out which type of undies makes you feel like a superhero and which ones leave you feeling like a...well, let's just say not a superhero.

Imagine yourself as an underpants explorer, venturing into the uncharted territory of your own wardrobe. You'll decipher the clues of leg length, material texture, and activity level, piecing together the puzzle of what makes the perfect pair. Is it all about breathability? Does support trump everything? These are the questions, young champions of comfort, that this chapter will help you answer!

Think of growing up as an epic quest, and your underwear is your secret armor. It's the foundation of your confidence, the hidden layer that keeps you cool, calm, and collected (or maybe just comfy enough to face the day). With great underpant power comes great responsibility (don't worry, it's more about choosing wisely than fighting evil villains!). This chapter will be your trusty guide, teaching you everything you ever wanted to know about picking the perfect pair, from the science behind fabric blends to the secrets of avoiding wedges.

So, are you ready to unlock the mysteries of your underwear drawer and become a master of underpants knowledge? Are you prepared to become a comfort crusader, a style savior, or a champion of personal choice? Remember, your underwear is your choice, and this chapter is here to help you navigate it with confidence, humor, and maybe even a little sock puppet action (because why not?).

We're entering the arena of the Great Underpants Showdown, where the mighty Boxers clash with the valiant Briefs in an epic battle for underwear supremacy. But fear not, young adventurer, for you won't be thrown into the mosh pit blindfolded. This chapter will be your trusty battle-ax, equipping you with the knowledge to choose your champion wisely.

First, let's meet the contenders:

Boxer, the Loose Canon: Picture a comfy pair of pajamas, except down there. Boxers offer freedom, breathability, and a laid-back swagger. Imagine yourself conquering Mount Coolitude in their breezy embrace, the wind playing your leg-hair symphony. But beware, loose can mean bunching, and bunching can be the enemy of smooth moves (and sometimes hygiene!).

Imagine a refreshing ocean breeze caressing your nether regions. Boxers, with their loose fit and airy fabrics, excel in breathability — perfect for hot summer days, intense sports sessions, or simply lounging around at home. But beware, young adventurer, excessive airflow can sometimes turn into unwanted exposure, especially during physical activity.

Brief, the Snug Gladiator:

Briefs offer support, security, and a sleek silhouette. Imagine yourself mastering the Monkey Bars of Confidence, their compression holding you firm. But remember, a tight grip can sometimes feel restrictive, and those wedgies? Let's just say they're not the stuff of legends.

Think of briefs as the ultimate support system for your undercarriage. Their snug fit keeps everything comfortably in place, ideal for high-impact sports, running, or any activity that requires stability. However, the trade-off? Reduced airflow can lead to discomfort and potential irritation, especially in warmer climates.

The Trunks of Fury:

These bad boys combine the leg freedom of boxers with a bit of brief-like snugness. Think of them as the ninja of the underpants world, stealthy and versatile. But be warned, they might not be for everyone's taste, and finding the right fit can be tricky.

Now, the choice is yours, young Padawan. But remember, this isn't a "one size fits all" battle. Consider your personal preferences, your daily activities, and even the weather (yes, even down there!). Do you crave the breezy comfort of a boxer on a lazy Saturday? Or the confidence-boosting snugness of a brief for that big game? The key is experimenting, exploring, and finding the combo that makes you feel like the ultimate underpants champion.

But wait, there's more! This chapter isn't just about picking sides. We'll also delve into the mysteries of:

Fabric Frenzy:

Cotton, polyester, and blends galore! We'll help you navigate the fabric jungle and find the material that makes your nether regions sing.

Care and Conquests: How often should you wash them? Can you put them in the dryer? Fear not, young warrior; we'll answer all your burning (and hopefully not itchy) questions.

The Rise of the Rebel:

What if boxers and briefs aren't your jam? Don't worry; we'll explore other options like boxer briefs, long johns, and even...dare we say it...going commando (but proceed with caution!).

Enter the boxer briefs and trunks, offering a middle ground between freedom and support. Boxer briefs provide more leg coverage than briefs while maintaining some breathability. On the other hand, trunks combine a shorter leg with a snug fit, perfect for those who desire support and a less restrictive feel.

But remember, comfort is subjective! What works for your best friend might not work for you. Consider your activity level, personal preferences, and even your body type. For example, briefs might be your best bet if you chafe easily. If you tend to overheat, boxers could be your savior.

Pro Tip: Experiment with different fabrics! Natural materials like cotton and linen offer superior breathability, while synthetic blends often wick away moisture and dry faster.

While both boxers and briefs have their merits, remember that proper hygiene is key, no matter your choice. Change your underpants daily, especially after sweating or participating in sports. Wash them according to the fabric care instructions (hot water for whites, cold for colors) and let them dry completely before storing. Ignoring these vital steps can lead to unpleasant odors, irritation, and even infections.

So, young warriors, remember: the Great Underpants Showdown isn't about mindlessly choosing a side. It's about understanding your needs, experimenting with different options, and finding the perfect balance between comfort, support, and hygiene. With the right knowledge and a little exploration, you'll claim your underpants destiny in no time!

10

FROM PEACH FUZZ TO BEARD: THE FACIAL HAIR TIMELINE

Feeling confused about the random hairs sprouting on your cheeks – are they friends or foes? Brace yourself, young adventurer, because you're about to embark on a thrilling quest: The Facial Hair Timeline! From wispy peach fuzz to the legendary full beard, this chapter will guide you through the uncharted territory of your own face, deciphering the mysteries of hair growth and discovering the secrets to grooming like a pro.

Forget boring lectures about follicles and hormones (although science is pretty cool, too!). This is about conquering the mysteries of your own face, like an explorer venturing into a wild jungle. We'll be tracking the evolution of your facial hair, from the first whispers of fuzz to the potential roar of a full beard. Is it magic? Superfood smoothies? Nope, it's the incredible (and sometimes confusing) process of growing up!

Imagine yourself as a facial hair archaeologist, excavating the hidden potential beneath your skin. You'll be deciphering the clues of genetics, hormones, and individual growth patterns, piecing together the puzzle of why your best friend sprouted a beard at 13 while you're still sporting a faint fuzz. Is it a sign of coolness? Superpowers in the making? These are the questions, young Padawans of facial hair evolution, that this chapter will help you answer!

Think of growing up as an epic quest, and your facial hair is the ultimate trophy. It's the symbol of changing times, a marker of maturity, and maybe even a source of future bragging rights (just ask your dad with his epic mustache!). But with great facial hair power comes great responsibility (don't worry, it's more about patience and self-care than bossing your chin hairs around!). This chapter will be your trusty guide, teaching you everything you need to know about navigating the exciting (and sometimes hilarious) changes on your face. From understanding your own growth pattern to mastering the art of basic grooming, you'll learn how to embrace your facial hair journey with confidence and maybe even a little bit of humor.

So, are you ready to unlock the secrets of your facial hair and become a master of its mysteries? Are you prepared to become a fuzz whisperer, a grooming guru, a champion of self-acceptance? Remember, your facial hair is unique and amazing, and this chapter is here to help you navigate its ups and downs with knowledge, humor, and maybe even a little bit of beard oil (because even future beards need care!).

Around the ages of 8 to 10, you may notice tiny, soft hairs on your upper lip, chin, and cheeks. This is often referred to as "peach fuzz" because it resembles the soft texture of a peach. Don't worry if it's barely noticeable initially; everyone starts from here!

Picture this: you're chilling in front of the mirror, and suddenly, you spot it – tiny, wispy hairs popping up like magic on your upper lip, chin, and cheeks. It's like someone sprinkled fairy dust on your face! You've entered the enchanted realm of peach fuzz paradise, where your face feels as soft as a fuzzy peach.

As you progress through puberty, usually between the ages of 11 and 14, your peach fuzz may thicken and darken. You might notice a slight shadow on your upper lip or the beginning of a few hairs sprouting on your chin. This stage is called the "stubble stage," and it's an exciting indicator of the changes happening in your body.

Fast forward a bit, and now you're rocking the stubble look! Those once delicate fuzzies have leveled up into a shadowy squad of stubble on your upper lip and chin. It's like your face is throwing a party, and everyone's invited – even those cheeky little hairs joining the fun!

As you continue through puberty, typically between the ages of 14 and 17, your facial hair might start growing more noticeably. However, it's common for it to come in unevenly or patchy at first. Some areas might have more hair growth than others, and that's completely normal! Embrace the patchiness and remember that everyone's facial hair journey is unique.

By the late teens and early twenties, many young men start to see their facial hair fill out more thoroughly. This is when you might achieve the coveted "full beard" look. Your facial hair will likely continue to thicken and grow in density over time, creating a distinct pattern that is unique to you.

Now, brace yourselves because it's time for the grand finale – the full beard fiesta! Your facial hair has grown up, graduated from stubble school, and is now throwing the ultimate party on your face. It's like a garden of manliness blossoming on your chin, cheeks, and everywhere in between. Cue the confetti – you've reached peak beard-dom!

As your facial hair becomes more prominent, taking care of it is essential. Regular grooming, including washing, trimming, and shaping, will help keep your beard looking neat and tidy. Experimenting with different styles can also be fun and allow you to express your individuality.

Remember, the facial hair timeline is different for everyone. Some boys may develop facial hair earlier or later than others, and the growth rate can vary greatly from person to person. Patience is critical during this process, as your facial hair will continue to evolve and change over time.

But hold your horses because with a great beard comes great responsibility – grooming galore! Regular washing, trimming, and shaping will keep that facial foliage in check. It's like giving your beard a spa day – because who says your face can't feel pampered, too?

From peach fuzz to beard, the facial hair timeline is an exciting and natural part of growing up. Embrace each stage of the journey, celebrate your uniqueness, and remember that your facial hair reflects your individuality and maturity. So, whether you're sporting a soft fuzz or a full-grown beard, wear it with pride and confidence!

11

BODY ODOR 101: THE BATTLE OF THE B.O.

Demystifying Body Odor & Conquering the B.O. Beast!

Ever wonder why sometimes you smell like a freshly cut rose, and other times...well, not so much? Brace yourselves, young adventurers, because we're diving headfirst into the sometimes fragrant, sometimes funky world of body odor! This isn't your boring biology class about sweat glands (although understanding them is helpful!). This is about understanding and conquering the dreaded B.O., turning you into a master of freshness and confidence.

This is about becoming a body odor detective, like Sherlock Holmes, cracking the case of the mysterious smell. We'll decipher the clues of sweat, bacteria, and even food, figuring out why exactly your body sometimes decides to play olfactory tricks. Is it magic? Super-spicy burritos? Nope, it's just science (don't worry, it's fun!).

Imagine yourself as a body odor explorer, venturing into the uncharted territory of your own skin. You'll be mapping out the sweat zones, identifying the friendly and not-so-friendly bacteria, and piecing together the puzzle of what makes your B.O. unique. Is it a sign of something wrong? Do you need to become a superhero for showering? These are the questions, young champions of hygiene, that this chapter will help you answer!

Think of growing up as an epic quest; your body odor is one of the challenges you'll face. But fear not! With proper knowledge and a few simple strategies, you can conquer the B.O. beast and emerge victorious (and smell fresh!). This chapter will be your trusty guide, teaching you everything you need to know about managing your body odor, from understanding the science behind sweat to mastering the art of good hygiene. You'll learn tips for staying fresh, choosing the right deodorant (because not all heroes wear capes; some wear cool deodorants!), and even dealing with those awkward gym locker moments.

So, are you ready to unlock the secrets of your body odor and become a master of freshness? Are you prepared to become a sweat whisperer, a hygiene hero, or a confidence champion? Remember, everyone experiences body odor, but understanding it and managing it empowers you to feel good and smell good, too. Let's explore it together, shall we? And, who knows, maybe you'll even discover that your unique scent is kind of like your own personal superpower!

Round 1: The Science of Sweat - Friend or Foe?

Alright, warriors of freshness, let's get down to the nitty-gritty! Before we unleash our arsenal of hygiene tips, we need to understand the enemy: sweat. Contrary to popular belief, sweat itself is actually odorless. Yes, you read that right! It's your body's natural cooling system, keeping you from turning into a human puddle on a hot day. So, where does the B.O. come from? Enter the stage, stage right... bacteria!

These tiny critters live happily on your skin, munching on the proteins and sugars present in your sweat. And guess what they create as a delicious byproduct? Stinky molecules! Different bacteria produce different smells, which is why everyone's B.O. has its own unique "aroma."

Sweating is good! It regulates your body temperature, removes toxins, and even helps fight infection. Don't be afraid to sweat; just be prepared to manage the aftermath.

Round 2: Identifying the B.O. Culprits - Food, Fun, and Funky Zones

Now, not all sweat is created equal. Certain factors can amp up your B.O. game, turning a faint whiff into a full-blown olfactory assault. Here are the top contenders:

Spicy Foods: Remember those super-flavorful burritos we mentioned? Turns out, the spices you love can linger in your sweat, creating an interesting (and not always pleasant) fragrance.

- Intense Exercise: The more you work out and sweat, the more opportunities for bacteria to party. This is why showering after exercise is key!

- Stress and Anxiety: Feeling stressed or anxious? Your body releases hormones that can trigger sweat production, leading to B.O. So, take a deep breath, young warrior, and chill out!

- "Funky Zones": Certain body areas, like the armpits, groin, and feet, have more sweat glands and harbor specific bacteria. These areas require extra attention during your hygiene routine.

Round 3: Conquering the B.O. Beast - Hygiene Hacks for Heroes

Alright, now that you know your enemy, it's time to fight back! Here are some essential weapons in your B.O.-busting arsenal:

- **Shower Power:** This might seem obvious, but regular showers (especially after sweating) are crucial. Use warm water and gentle soap, focusing on the "funky zones."

- **Deodorant vs. Antiperspirant:** Deodorants mask odors, while antiperspirants block sweat production. Choose the one that best suits your needs.

- **Natural Solutions:** Baking soda, apple cider vinegar, and even lemon juice can be used as natural deodorants. Experiment to find what works for you.

- **Clothing Choices**: Breathable fabrics like cotton allow your skin to breathe, reducing sweat build-up and B.O.

- **Diet:** While you can't completely eliminate B.O.-causing foods, limiting spicy and processed options can help.

Remember, conquering B.O. is a journey, not a destination. There will be good days and not-so-good days. But with knowledge, hygiene habits, and a positive attitude, you can be the master of your own freshness and smell like a champion every day!

Round 4: Beyond the Basics - Advanced B.O. Tactics for True Champions

Alright, hygiene heroes, feeling fresh and confident? Time to graduate from deodorant basics and delve into the advanced tactics of B.O. management. Remember, mastering your personal aroma is like training for a marathon, not a sprint. Consistency and exploration are key!

Listen to your body! Everyone's B.O. is unique, so experiment and find what works best for you. What might be a miracle solution for your best friend might leave you smelling like a forgotten gym sock.

Weaponizing Your Wardrobe:

- Fabric Fighters: Synthetic fabrics trap sweat and odors, while natural fibers like cotton and linen promote breathability. Invest in breathable clothing, especially for workouts and hot weather.

- Layer Like a Ninja: Layering allows for easy adjustment throughout the day. Remove a sweaty outer layer to stay fresh, or add a light jacket to prevent excessive sweating.

- Shoe Savvy: Choose breathable shoes and rotate them regularly to allow them to air out. Consider using shoe inserts that absorb moisture and neutralize odors.

Diet Do's and Don'ts:

1. Hydration Hero: Drinking plenty of water flushes toxins and keeps your body functioning optimally, reducing B.O. potential.

2. Spice it Up (Strategically): While some spices can be B.O. villains, others, like ginger and parsley, have odor-fighting properties. Experiment and find your flavorful balance.

3. Limit the Culprits: Processed foods, sugary drinks, and excessive red meat can contribute to B.O. Opt for fresh fruits, vegetables, and whole grains to fuel your body and your freshness.

The Hygiene Arsenal Expands:

Exfoliation Power:

Regularly exfoliating removes dead skin cells, where bacteria love to party, reducing potential B.O. Choose gentle exfoliators suitable for your skin type.

Footcare Frenzy:

Don't neglect your feet! Wash them daily, dry them thoroughly, and consider using foot powder or antiperspirant sprays to keep them feeling fresh.

The Power of Prevention:

Address potential medical conditions contributing to excessive sweating or B.O., such as hormonal imbalances or thyroid issues. Consult a doctor if you have concerns.

Remember, true B.O. mastery is a journey of self-discovery. Embrace the exploration, experiment with different solutions, and don't be afraid to ask for help from parents, doctors, or even your cool older sibling (if you have one!). With dedication and a dash of humor, you'll conquer the B.O. beast and emerge as a champion of freshness, ready to face the world with confidence (and a pleasant aroma)!

So, young warriors, are you ready to unlock the next level of your B.O. management skills? Grab your knowledge and your favorite deodorant (or natural alternative!), and let's embark on this fresh adventure together! Remember, feeling good about yourself starts with feeling fresh, and conquering B.O. is just one step in your epic journey of self-discovery.

12

THE SCOOP ON SWEAT: STAYING FRESH

Welcome to a chapter all about something we're sure you're familiar with – sweat! Yep, that's right – that cool, sticky stuff that sometimes shows up when you're running around, playing tag, or even just chilling on a hot day. But fear not because we've got the inside scoop on sweat, how it works, and how to stay fresh as a daisy even when things heat up.

First off, let's talk about why we sweat. You see, sweat is like our body's built-in air conditioning system. When we get hot from running around or when it's warm outside, our body starts to sweat to help us cool down. It's like our body's way of saying, "Phew, it's getting toasty in here – time to turn on the sprinklers!"

But wait, there's more! Did you know that sweat isn't just water? Nope, it's a mix of water, salt, and other stuff our body doesn't need. So, when you sweat, you're not just losing water – you're also getting rid of some extra salt and other icky stuff that your body doesn't want to hang around. Pretty cool, right?

Now, you might wonder, "But hey, if sweat is so great at cooling us down, why does it sometimes make us smell a bit funky?" Ah, excellent question, my young padawans! When sweat mixes with bacteria on our skin, it can create a not-so-pleasant odor. But fear not – that's where good ol' soap and water come to the rescue!

Yep, you heard that right – good old-fashioned hygiene is the secret to staying fresh as a daisy. So, make sure you hop in the shower regularly, especially after a sweaty adventure or a particularly intense game of soccer. And don't forget to scrub behind your ears and in all those nooks and crannies – because bacteria love to hang out in those sneaky spots!

Oh, and here's another fun fact – did you know that some people sweat more than others? It's true! Factors like genetics, hormones, and even the weather can all affect how much we sweat. So, if you find yourself sweating buckets while your friend barely breaks a sweat, don't worry – it's totally normal!

Now, let's talk about sweat and sports. When you're playing sports or running around like a wild tornado, you're bound to work up a sweat – and that's a good thing! But it's also important to stay hydrated by drinking plenty of water, especially on hot days or during intense activities. Think of water as your body's best friend – it helps keep you cool, hydrated, and ready to tackle whatever adventure comes your way!

But hey, even superheroes need a little extra help sometimes, right? That's where deodorant comes in! Yep, you heard that right – deodorant is like your secret weapon against sweat and odor. Just a quick swipe under your arms in the morning can help keep you feeling fresh and confident all day.

And speaking of confidence, let's talk about how to handle those awkward moments when sweat makes a surprise appearance – like during a big presentation at school or when you're meeting new friends. Remember, sweating is totally normal and nothing to be embarrassed about. So, take a deep breath, dab away any excess sweat with a tissue or towel, and rock on like your superstar!

Now, let's delve a little deeper into some sweat-related myths and mysteries. Have you ever heard someone say that sweating can make you lose weight? Well, here's the truth: while sweating can temporarily help you lose a little water weight, it's not a magic solution for shedding pounds. The real key to staying healthy and fit is eating a balanced diet, staying active, and taking care of your body – sweat or no sweat!

And hey, speaking of myths, let's bust another one while we're at it. You might have heard that sweat is actually stinky. But guess what? Sweat itself doesn't actually smell– the bacteria on our skin mingle with sweat and create that distinctive odor. So, next time you catch a whiff of that not-so-fresh scent, just remember – blame it on the bacteria!

Now, let's talk about some fun ways to stay cool and fresh when the temperature rises. Ever tried a water balloon fight on a hot summer day? Or how about running through the sprinklers in your backyard? These are not only super fun ways to beat the heat but also give you a chance to cool down and let your body do its thing – sweating included!

And hey, here's a pro tip for all you adventurous souls out there: try freezing some watermelon chunks or grapes for a refreshing snack on those scorching summer days. Not only are they delicious, but they'll also help keep you hydrated and cool as a cucumber – or should we say, cool as a frozen watermelon chunk!

But wait, there's more. Have you ever heard of a "sweat lodge"? It's a traditional Native American practice where people sit in a small hut and sweat out toxins as part of a purification ceremony. Pretty cool, huh? While you might not have a sweat lodge in your backyard, you can still create your own mini version by turning your bathroom into a steam room – just crank up the hot water in the shower, close the door, and let the steam work its magic. Just remember to stay hydrated and take breaks if you start to feel too hot!

13

LOCKER ROOM BLUES: DEALING WITH BODY IMAGE

Now, let's start by briefly getting real. Have you ever looked around the locker room and compared yourself to the other kids? Maybe you noticed someone who seemed taller, stronger, or more muscular than you – and suddenly, that little voice in your head started whispering doubts and insecurities. Sound familiar? Well, fear not – you're not alone!

You see, it's normal to feel a little self-conscious sometimes, especially when surrounded by other kids who seem to have it all figured out. But here's the thing – everyone's body is different, which makes you unique and awesome in your own special way.

So, the next time you find yourself in the locker room blues, remember that your worth isn't determined by how you look or compare to others. Whether you're tall, short, skinny, or muscular, you're a superstar just the way you are – and don't forget it!

Let's talk about some fun ways to boost your body confidence and rock that locker room like a boss. Ever tried striking a power pose in front of the mirror? It might sound silly, but standing tall with your hands on your hips can actually make you feel more confident and powerful – try it out and see for yourself!

And speaking of mirrors, here's a little secret: how you see yourself in the mirror isn't always how others see you. Yep, it's true! We're often our own harshest critics, but chances are, your friends and classmates see you as the awesome, amazing person you are – flaws and all!

Now, let's talk about the power of positive self-talk. Instead of focusing on what you wish you could change about your body, try celebrating all the amazing things it can do! Whether you're scoring goals on the soccer field, taking that math test, or making your friends laugh with your epic jokes, your body is capable of some pretty incredible stuff – and that's worth celebrating!

And hey, here's a little reminder for those moments when the locker room blues start to creep in: you are so much more than just your appearance. Whether you're smart, funny, kind, or creative, you've got a whole bunch of awesome qualities that make you who you are – and that's what truly matters.

You might have heard that only certain types of bodies are considered attractive – but guess what? Beauty comes in all shapes, sizes, and colors! Whether you're tall, short, curvy, or slim, there's no one-size-fits-all definition of beauty. So, embrace your unique features and celebrate what makes you, well, you!

And hey, speaking of myths, let's bust another one while we're at it. You might have heard that you need to look a certain way to be happy or successful – but here's the truth: happiness and success come from within, not from how you look on the outside. So, focus on being the best version of yourself, inside and out, and the rest will fall into place.

Now, let's talk about the power of surrounding yourself with positive influences. Whether it's friends who lift you up, family members who love you unconditionally, or mentors who inspire you to be your best self, having a support system can make all the difference when it comes to feeling confident and comfortable in your own skin.

And hey, here's a little secret: everyone has their own insecurities – even those who seem to have it all together. Yep, it's true! So, the next time you feel down about yourself, remember you're not alone. We're all in this together, navigating the ups and downs of growing up and figuring out who we are along the way.

Let's talk about some fun ways to boost your body confidence and banish those locker room blues for good. Have you ever tried practicing positive affirmations? It might sound cheesy, but repeating positive statements like "I am strong, I am capable, I am worthy" can actually help retrain your brain to focus on the good instead of the negative.

And speaking of positivity, let's talk about the power of self-care. Whether it's taking a bubble bath, going for a walk in nature, or indulging in your favorite hobby, taking time to care for yourself can do wonders for your mental and emotional well-being. So, make self-care a priority and watch as your confidence soars!

True confidence isn't about achieving a specific look; it's about accepting and appreciating your body for what it is: a strong, capable, and unique vessel for your awesome self. This chapter is just the beginning of your journey to body positivity. Use these strategies to break free from myths, embrace your individuality, and conquer the world with confidence radiating from within!

Myth	Reality Check	Confidence Booster
My body needs to look a certain way to be "cool" or accepted.	Nope! Coolness comes from within, from your personality, talents, and how you treat others. True friends will accept you just as you are.	Focus on what makes you unique and awesome! Develop your passions, be kind, and embrace your individuality. That's where true coolness lies.
There's a "perfect" body type everyone should strive for.	Absolutely not! Bodies come in all shapes and sizes, and they're all amazing! What matters most is being healthy and feeling good about yourself.	Celebrate your body's diversity! Appreciate its strength, agility, and all the incredible things it allows you to do. There's no "perfect" body, just different bodies doing amazing things.

Comparing myself to others will motivate me to change.	Comparing yourself to others is a recipe for unhappiness. Everyone's on their own unique journey and focusing on someone else's progress will only hinder your own.	Focus on your own goals and celebrate your personal achievements. Be your own motivation, not someone else's highlight reel.
If I exercise and eat healthy, I'll automatically have the ideal body.	Health and fitness are crucial for feeling good, but they don't guarantee a specific appearance. Everybody responds differently to exercise and diet.	Move your body because it feels good and energizes you, not to achieve a certain look. Eat healthy to nourish your body from the inside out, not to mold it into an unrealistic image.
Feeling insecure about my body means I'm weak or vain.	Feeling insecure about your body is totally normal, especially during the crazy changes of growing up. It's not about weakness; it's about navigating a complex world.	Talk to someone you trust about your feelings, and seek support from friends, family, or even a counselor. Remember, you're not alone, and there's no shame in asking for help.

Now, let's address the elephant in the room – social media. While platforms like Instagram and TikTok can be fun and entertaining, they can also be a breeding ground for comparison and self-doubt.

So, the next time you find yourself scrolling through your feed and feeling less-than-awesome, remember this: what you see online isn't always the full picture. People tend to post their highlight reels, not their behind-the-scenes struggles. So, take everything you see with a grain of salt and focus on living your best life offline.

And finally, let's talk about the importance of being kind to yourself. We're often our own toughest critics, but treating ourselves with the same kindness and compassion that we would show a friend is crucial. So, the next time you catch yourself thinking negative thoughts about your body or appearance, try flipping the script and focusing on all the things that make you awesome instead.

So, the next time you face the locker room blues, remember this: you are amazing, unique, and worthy of love and acceptance just the way you are. So go ahead, rock that locker room like the superstar you are – because you, my friend, are absolutely unstoppable!

14

MASTERING THE ART OF SHAVING

Hey there, future gentlemen! Welcome to a chapter all about one of the most iconic rituals of manhood – shaving. Yep, we're diving into the world of razors, shaving cream, and that oh-so-satisfying feeling of a smooth, clean shave. So, grab your shaving gear and get ready to master the art of shaving like a pro!

First, let's talk about why we shave in the first place. For many guys, shaving is a rite of passage, a symbol of maturity, and a way to keep our faces looking fresh and clean. Whether you're sporting a peach fuzz mustache or a full-on beard, knowing how to shave properly is an essential skill every gentleman should master.

You might be wondering, "But hey, when should I start shaving?" Well, here's the scoop: there's no one-size-fits-all answer. Some guys start shaving as early as their teens, while others wait until their twenties – and that's totally okay! The key is listening to your body and shaving when you feel ready.

Okay, so you've decided it's time to take the plunge and start shaving – but where do you begin? Fear not, my young apprentices, because we've got you covered. The first step is choosing the right tools for the job. Whether you prefer a classic safety razor, a modern cartridge razor, or an electric shaver, there's a shaving tool out there to suit your style and preferences.

Next up, let's talk about shaving cream. Think of shaving cream as your trusty sidekick – it helps soften your stubble, lubricate your skin, and prevent irritation and razor burn. So, grab your favorite shaving cream – whether it's a rich, luxurious foam or a silky, smooth gel – and get ready to lather up like a pro.

Now, onto the main event – the actual shaving process. But wait, before diving in headfirst, there are a few important tips to remember. First, always shave after showering or washing your face with warm water. This helps soften your hair and open up your pores, making getting a close, comfortable shave easier.

Next, make sure you're using gentle, steady strokes with your razor, and always shave in the direction your hair grows. This helps minimize irritation and reduce the risk of nicks and cuts. And remember – there's no need to apply too much pressure. Let the weight of the razor do the work for you.

And speaking of nicks and cuts, let's talk about handling those pesky little mishaps. If you do happen to nick yourself while shaving, don't panic! Simply rinse the area with cold water to help stop the bleeding, apply a small amount of aftershave or aloe vera gel to soothe the skin, and voila – you're back in action!

Now, let's talk about the finishing touches – aftershave. Not only does aftershave smell great, but it also helps soothe your skin, reduce inflammation, and prevent ingrown hairs. So, grab your favorite aftershave lotion or balm, splash it on your face like a boss, and get ready to feel refreshed and revitalized.

Shaving isn't just about removing unwanted hair – it's also a chance to pamper yourself and indulge in a little self-care. So, why not turn your shaving routine into a mini spa session? Light some candles, play your favorite tunes, and take your time – because you deserve it, champ!

Now that you've mastered the basics of shaving let's talk about some advanced techniques to take your shaving game to the next level. Have you ever heard of shaving with the grain versus against the grain? Here's the scoop: shaving with the direction your hair grows (aka "with the grain") can help minimize irritation and reduce the risk of ingrown hairs. But if you're looking for an extra-close shave, you can try shaving against the grain – just be sure to do so with caution to avoid irritation.

And hey, speaking of advanced techniques, let's talk about the art of the perfect shave. It's all about precision, attention to detail, and a little bit of finesse. Start by mapping out the direction your hair grows using your fingers or a small comb. Then, use short, controlled strokes to carefully shave each section of your face, taking care to rinse your razor frequently and reapply shaving cream as needed.

Now, let's address the elephant in the room – razor bumps and ingrown hairs. You're not alone if you've ever experienced these pesky little bumps after shaving! But fear not – there are plenty of tricks to help prevent and treat them. First, try exfoliating your skin regularly to remove dead skin cells and prevent hair follicles from becoming clogged. You can also try using a sharp, clean razor and avoiding shaving too closely to the skin to minimize irritation.

And hey, here's a pro tip for all you shaving enthusiasts out there: try shaving in the shower! The steam and warm water help soften your hair and open up your pores, making it easier to get a close, comfortable shave. Plus, it's a great way to save time and streamline your grooming routine – talk about a win-win!

Now, let's talk about shaving frequency. How often should you shave? Well, that depends on your personal preference and the rate of your hair growth. Some guys prefer to shave daily for that smooth, clean-shaven look, while others opt for a more laid-back approach and shave every few days. Experiment with different schedules to find what works best for you and your skin.

And speaking of skin, let's talk about post-shave care. Once you've finished shaving, rinse your face with cold water to help close your pores, then pat your skin dry with a clean towel. Follow up with a hydrating moisturizer or aftershave lotion to soothe your skin and keep it feeling soft and supple.

Mastering the art of shaving is all about practice, patience, and a little bit of experimentation. Whether you're a shaving novice or a seasoned pro, remember to take your time, use the right tools for the job, and pamper your skin with some post-shave TLC. So, grab your razor, lather up, and get ready to shave like a boss!

15

HANDS-ON GUIDE TO GROOMING

Ever look in the mirror and feel like your hair is channeling Einstein after a windstorm, your nails could rival Wolverine's claws, and your face needs a spa day more than your grandma? Relax! This chapter isn't here to judge your current grooming routine (or lack thereof). It's here to be your ultimate wingman, equipping you with the knowledge and tools to transform yourself from a "messy masterpiece" to a "polished prince" (or whatever version of awesome you're aiming for).

Forget boring lectures about hygiene (although knowing why washing your hands is cool is pretty neat). This is about controlling your image, like a superhero mastering their superpowers. We'll be diving into hair, nails, skincare, and even a few secret weapons to help you feel confident and comfortable in your own skin (and avoid making your mom faint from...well, let's just say not-so-pleasant odors).

Imagine yourself as a grooming guru, venturing into the uncharted territory of your bathroom cabinet. You'll decipher the mysteries of shampoos, clippers, and face washes, figuring out what works best for your unique style and needs. Is it all about the slicked-back hair and fancy cologne? Or maybe the laid-back surfer vibes and natural look? These are the questions, young champions of self-care, that this chapter will help you answer!

Think of growing up as an epic quest; your grooming routine is your personal armor. It's the foundation of your confidence, the shield against awkward moments, and the key to unlocking the "cool kid" within (even if you're secretly a huge Star Wars nerd at heart). With great grooming power comes great responsibility (don't worry, it's more about learning what works than becoming a superhero). This chapter will be your trusty guide, teaching you everything you need to know about conquering your bathroom cabinet, mastering basic grooming techniques, and maybe even picking up a few pro tips to impress your friends (or crush!).

So, are you ready to unleash your inner grooming master? Grab your metaphorical battle-axe (or maybe just a comb and toothbrush), flip the page, and let's embark on this hilarious and informative journey together!

Whether you're getting ready for a big event, a special occasion, or just another day at school, knowing how to groom yourself like a pro is an essential skill every guy should master. So, grab your grooming gear and get ready to dive into the wonderful world of personal care!

Let's start with the basics – grooming tools. Every grooming guru needs a few essential tools, including a comb or brush, a toothbrush and toothpaste, nail clippers, and tweezers. These tools will help you keep your hair, teeth, nails, and eyebrows looking neat and tidy – because, let's face it, nobody likes a messy mane or unkempt nails!

Now, let's talk about hair care. Whether you're rocking a buzz cut, a crew cut, or a flowing mane of locks, taking care of your hair is key to looking and feeling your best. Start by washing your hair regularly with a gentle shampoo and conditioner to keep it clean and healthy. And don't forget to comb or brush your hair regularly to prevent tangles and keep it looking neat and tidy.

Next up, let's talk about oral hygiene. Taking care of your teeth and gums is essential for a healthy smile and fresh breath. So, make sure you brush your teeth at least twice a day, using a fluoride toothpaste and a soft-bristled toothbrush. Don't forget to floss daily to remove plaque and food particles from between your teeth – your dentist will thank you!

Now, let's address the elephant in the room – body odor (something we already know a lot about). Yep, it's a fact of life, but fear not – there are plenty of ways to keep yourself smelling fresh as a daisy. Start by showering regularly, using soap and water to wash away sweat, dirt, and bacteria. And don't forget to use deodorant or antiperspirant to help control odor and keep your underarms feeling dry and fresh.

And speaking of showers, let's talk about skincare. Taking care of your skin is important for preventing acne, reducing oiliness, and keeping your complexion clear and healthy. So, ensure you wash your face with a gentle cleanser every day, followed by a moisturizer with SPF to protect your skin from the sun's harmful rays.

Ever heard of exfoliation? It's like giving your skin a deep clean, removing dead skin cells, and leaving your complexion looking fresh and radiant. You can use a gentle exfoliating scrub or a facial brush to gently buff away dull skin and reveal a smoother, brighter complexion.

And speaking of skincare, let's talk about moisturizing. Hydrated skin is happy skin, so make sure you moisturize regularly to keep your skin soft, smooth, and supple. Look for a moisturizer that's suited to your skin type – whether you have dry, oily, or sensitive skin – and apply it generously after cleansing to lock in moisture and keep your skin looking its best.

Next up, let's talk about grooming your eyebrows. Yep, those little patches of hair above your eyes need some attention, too! Use a pair of tweezers to pluck any stray hairs and shape your brows to your desired shape. Just remember to go easy – less is more when it comes to eyebrow grooming, and you don't want to end up with sparse or over-plucked brows!

Now, let's talk about the art of the perfect shave. Whether you prefer a clean shave, or a rugged stubble look, getting a close, comfortable shave is all about technique. Start by washing your face with warm water to soften your hair and open up your pores, then apply a generous amount of shaving cream or gel to lubricate your skin and help prevent irritation. Use short, gentle strokes with a sharp razor to shave in the direction of your hair growth, rinsing your razor frequently to remove any buildup. And don't forget to finish off with a soothing aftershave lotion or balm to calm your skin and keep it feeling refreshed.

Now, let's talk about fragrance. A good cologne or body spray can be the perfect finishing touch to your grooming routine, making you feel fresh and confident all day. Choose a scent that reflects your personality and style – whether you prefer something light and citrusy or bold and woody – and apply it sparingly to pulse points like your wrists, neck, and chest for maximum impact.

And finally, let's talk about confidence. Because here's the thing – grooming isn't just about looking good on the outside; it's also about feeling good on the inside. So, stand tall, rock your unique style, and remember that true confidence comes from within. Whether you're rocking a fresh haircut, a clean shave, or a killer outfit, the most attractive thing you can wear is a smile – so wear it proudly, my friend!

By mastering the basics, experimenting with advanced techniques, and embracing your unique style, you can look and feel your best every single day. So go ahead – unleash your inner grooming guru, and get ready to conquer the world with style, confidence, and a whole lot of swaggers!

16

THE ABCS OF ACNE AND HOW TO COMBAT IT

Yo, warriors of smooth skin! Have pesky pimples taken over your once-flawless face, turning your selfies into a minefield of unwanted red dots? Don't despair, brave adventurers! This chapter is your arsenal against the dreaded acne beast, packed with knowledge, tips, and strategies to help you reclaim your skin's glory. Forget boring lectures about hormones and clogged pores (although understanding them helps!). This is about becoming an acne detective, like Sherlock Holmes unraveling the mystery of your breakouts. We'll decipher the clues of diet, stress, and even genetics, figuring out what's triggering your blemishes and how to fight back. Is it magic? Superfood smoothies? It's science (the fun kind!) combined with a healthy dose of self-care.

Imagine yourself as an acne archaeologist, venturing into the uncharted territory of your own face. You'll be mapping out the breakout zones, identifying the sneaky culprits, and piecing together the puzzle of what makes your acne unique. Is it a sign of the end of the world? Do you need to become a superhero of skincare? These are the questions, young champions of clear skin, that this chapter will help you answer!

Think of growing up as an epic quest; your acne is just one of the challenges you'll face. But fear not! With the right knowledge and a few simple strategies, you can banish those blemishes and emerge victorious (and glowing!). This chapter will be your trusty guide, teaching you everything you need to know about understanding acne, from the science behind breakouts to mastering gentle cleansing routines and choosing the right products (because not all heroes wear capes; some wear acne-fighting creams!). You'll learn tips for staying calm (stress can be a breakout trigger!), navigating the sometimes confusing world of skincare labels, and even dealing with those awkward "mirror moments."

So, are you ready to unlock the secrets of your acne and become a master of clear skin? Are you prepared to become a pimple whisperer, a skincare guru, and self-confidence champion? Everyone experiences acne, but understanding and managing it empowers you to feel good and look your best. Let's explore it together, shall we? And who knows, maybe you'll even discover that conquering acne is like defeating a villain in your own personal superhero movie!

Your Personal Acne Action Plan: Handy Checklist

Okay, warriors, now that you're pumped to banish those breakouts, here's a handy checklist to keep track of your progress and personalize your acne-fighting strategies:

Challenge	Action Step	Pro Tip
Identify your triggers:	Track your breakouts in a journal, noting diet, stress levels, and skincare products used.	Pay attention to patterns: certain foods, lack of sleep, or harsh cleansers could be culprits.
Wash gently but regularly:	Wash your face twice daily (morning and night) with lukewarm water and a gentle cleanser.	Avoid harsh soaps or scrubbing, as they can irritate your skin and worsen breakouts.
Moisturize, don't fry:	Use a lightweight, oil-free moisturizer to keep your skin hydrated and healthy.	Dry skin can overproduce oil, leading to more breakouts.
Hands off the face:	Resist the urge to touch, pick, or pop your pimples!	This can spread bacteria and worsen inflammation.
Seek professional help (if needed):	If your acne is severe or persistent, consult a dermatologist for personalized advice and treatment options.	Don't hesitate to seek professional help – they're the acne-fighting champions!

Whether you're dealing with a few pesky pimples or a full-blown breakout, understanding the ABCs of acne is the first step towards achieving clear, healthy skin. So, grab your skincare arsenal and get ready to tackle those blemishes head-on!

Let's start with the basics – what exactly is acne? Acne is a skin condition that occurs when hair follicles become clogged with oil and dead skin cells, leading to the formation of pimples, blackheads, and whiteheads. It's most commonly found on the face, neck, chest, and back but can also appear on other body parts.

Now, let's talk about the different types of acne. First, we have white and blackheads – these are the most common types of acne and occur when hair follicles become clogged with oil and dead skin cells. Whiteheads appear as small, white bumps on the skin, while blackheads appear as dark spots on the skin's surface.

Next, we have papules and pustules – these are inflamed pimples that occur when the walls of hair follicles become ruptured, causing redness, swelling, and pus-filled lesions. These types of acne can be painful and tender to the touch and may leave behind scars if not treated properly.

And finally, we have cysts and nodules – these are the most severe types of acne and occur when deep, inflamed lesions form beneath the skin's surface. Cysts are pus-filled lesions that are often painful and may cause scarring, while nodules are hard, painful lumps that develop deep within the skin.

Now that we've covered the basics of acne let's talk about how to combat it. The first step is establishing a good skincare routine. This means washing your face twice daily with a gentle cleanser to remove excess oil, dirt, and bacteria from the skin's surface. Be sure to choose skincare products that are non-comedogenic and oil-free to prevent clogged pores and breakouts.

Next, let's talk about exfoliation. Exfoliating your skin regularly helps remove dead skin cells and unclog pores, preventing acne from forming. You can use a gentle exfoliating scrub or a chemical exfoliant containing ingredients like salicylic acid or glycolic acid to keep your skin looking fresh and clear.

And speaking of ingredients, let's talk about acne-fighting powerhouse ingredients. Look for skincare products containing ingredients like benzoyl peroxide, salicylic acid, and retinoids – these ingredients help kill acne-causing bacteria, unclog pores, and promote skin cell turnover, leading to clearer, healthier skin.

Now, let's talk about spot treatments. Despite our best efforts, acne sometimes manages to rear its ugly head. That's where spot treatments come in handy – these targeted treatments contain ingredients like benzoyl peroxide or salicylic acid to help dry out pimples and reduce inflammation, helping them heal faster.

And finally, let's talk about lifestyle factors. Believe it or not, things like diet, stress, and sleep can all play a role in the development of acne. So, eat a balanced diet rich in fruits, vegetables, and whole grains, practice stress-relief techniques like yoga or meditation, and aim for 7-9 hours of quality sleep each night to keep your skin looking its best.

Acne may be a common skin woe, but it's not something you have to live with forever. By understanding the ABCs of acne and adopting a comprehensive skincare routine, you can take control of your skin's health and achieve the clear, healthy complexion you've always dreamed of. So go ahead – say goodbye to blemishes and hello to radiant, confident skin!

17

NAVIGATING WET DREAMS AND BEYOND

Hey there, adventurers! Welcome to a chapter all about a natural and totally normal part of growing up – wet dreams. Whether you've experienced one already or are just curious about what to expect, understanding wet dreams and navigating them confidently is key to feeling comfortable in your changing body. So, let's dive in and explore this exciting aspect of puberty together!

First things first – what exactly is a wet dream? Well, a wet dream, also known as nocturnal emission, is when a guy ejaculates (or releases semen) during sleep. Yep, it's like mini fireworks show in your pants while catching some Z's! And guess what? It's totally normal and nothing to be embarrassed about.

Now, you might wonder, "Why do we dreams happen?" Great question! Wet dreams occur when your body produces more semen than it can hold, and the excess semen needs to be released. If you catch our drift, it's like your body's way of keeping things running smoothly and making sure your pipes don't get clogged.

But here's the thing – wet dreams aren't just a physical phenomenon; they can also be accompanied by intense dreams or fantasies that may involve sexual experiences. And that's totally normal, too! As your body goes through puberty and your hormones go haywire, it's natural to have all sorts of wild and wacky dreams – including some that might leave you feeling a little hot and bothered.

Now, let's talk about how to handle wet dreams like a pro. First, remember that wet dreams are a sign that your body is functioning perfectly and doing exactly what it's supposed to do. So, don't freak out or feel ashamed if you have one – it's just your body's way of keeping things in check.

Next, let's talk about what to do if you wake up in the middle of a wet dream. First off, take a deep breath and try not to panic. It's totally normal to feel a little surprised or confused but remember – wet dreams are nothing to be ashamed of. Simply clean yourself up, change your underwear if needed, and go back to sleep like nothing happened. Chances are, nobody else will even know!

Now, let's address the elephant in the room – talking about wet dreams with others. It can feel awkward or embarrassing to discuss something so personal with friends, family, or even your doctor. But here's the thing – talking about wet dreams can actually be really helpful and reassuring. So, if you have questions or concerns, don't hesitate to reach out to a trusted adult or healthcare professional for guidance and support.

And finally, let's talk about the bigger picture – puberty and growing up. Wet dreams are just one small part of the amazing journey your body is going through as you transition from boyhood to manhood. So, embrace the changes, celebrate your body's incredible abilities, and remember – you're not alone on this adventure. We're all in this together, navigating the ups and downs of puberty and discovering what it means to be a grown-up.

First up, let's address the age-old question – do wet dreams mean you're having naughty thoughts or watching inappropriate stuff? The answer is a resounding no! Wet dreams are a natural and involuntary bodily response, and they have nothing to do with your thoughts or behaviors while awake. So, rest assured – having a wet dream doesn't make you a bad person or mean you're doing anything wrong.

You might be wondering, "How often do wet dreams happen?" Well, there's no one-size-fits-all answer to this question. Some guys have wet dreams frequently, while others may never experience one – and both scenarios are normal. Wet dreams tend to happen more often during puberty when your hormones are in overdrive, but they can occur at any age.

Now, let's talk about prevention. You might be wondering if there's anything you can do to prevent wet dreams from happening. Well, the truth is, wet dreams are a natural and unavoidable part of growing up, and there's no surefire way to stop them from occurring. However, there are some things you can do to minimize their frequency, such as avoiding stimulating activities before bed, practicing relaxation techniques like deep breathing or meditation, and wearing loose-fitting underwear to allow for better airflow.

And finally, let's talk about the emotional side of wet dreams. You might be feeling a little embarrassed, confused, or even guilty after experiencing a wet dream – and that's totally normal. But here's the thing – wet dreams are nothing to be ashamed of, and they certainly don't define who you are as a person. So, be kind to yourself, permit yourself to feel whatever emotions come up, and remember – you're not alone. Every guy goes through this experience at some point, and there's nothing to be ashamed of.

Just remember, wet dreams are a natural and normal part of growing up, and nothing to be embarrassed or ashamed of. By understanding what wet dreams are, how they happen, and how to navigate them confidently and grace, you can embrace this aspect of puberty with ease and self-assurance. So go ahead – dream big, sleep tight, and enjoy the incredible journey of self-discovery ahead!

18

CRUSH CHRONICLES: UNDERSTANDING RELATIONSHIPS

We are entering a very exciting phase of your growth- one of the most exciting, confusing, and downright exhilarating aspects of growing up – relationships. Whether you've got a crush, are navigating the murky waters of dating, or are just curious about what it all means, understanding relationships is key to building strong connections and finding happiness in the world of romance. So, grab your heart-shaped sunglasses and prepare to embark on a journey through the wild and wonderful world of Crush Chronicles!

First things first – let's talk about crushes. Ah, crushes – those fluttery feelings you get when you can't stop thinking about someone special. Whether it's the cute girl in your math class or the charming guy on your soccer team, crushes are a natural and normal part of growing up. They can make you feel giddy, nervous, and downright euphoric – but they can also be a little confusing and overwhelming at times.

Now, you might wonder, "What exactly is a crush?" A crush is simply a strong, infatuated attraction to someone else. It's that feeling you get when you can't help but smile whenever you see them or when your heart skips a beat every time they walk into the room. Crushes can be fleeting and intense, or they can linger for weeks, months, or even years – but either way, they're a natural part of the human experience.

Next up, let's talk about dating. Dating is like a romantic adventure – it's an opportunity to get to know someone better, share experiences together, and see if you're compatible as a couple. Whether it's going out for ice cream, taking a stroll in the park, or catching a movie together, dating is all about spending quality time with someone special and building a connection.

Now, you might wonder, "How do I know if someone likes me back?" Well, that's the million-dollar question, isn't it? While it's not always easy to tell if someone likes you romantically, there are a few telltale signs to look out for. Does the person try to spend time with you, laugh at your jokes, or show interest in your hobbies and interests? These could be signs that they're crushing on you too!

But here's the thing – not every crush will turn into a relationship, and that's okay. Sometimes, crushes are just meant to be enjoyed from afar, without any expectations or pressure. And hey, even if things don't work out with your crush, that doesn't mean you're doomed to a life of singledom. There are plenty of fish in the sea, and you never know when you might stumble upon your next great love story!

Now, let's talk about communication. Whether you're flirting with your crush, asking someone out on a date, or navigating the ups and downs of a relationship. It's important to be open, honest, and respectful in your interactions with others and to express your thoughts, feelings, and desires openly and authentically. Remember – nobody's a mind reader, so don't be afraid to speak up and share what's on your mind!

And finally, let's talk about the most important relationship of all – the one you have with yourself. Before you can genuinely connect with someone else, it's essential to love and accept yourself just as you are. So, take the time to get to know yourself, pursue your passions, and build a life that brings you joy and fulfillment – because when you're happy and confident in who you are, you'll naturally attract the right people into your life.

Relationships are a beautiful, messy, and endlessly fascinating part of the human experience. Whether you're crushing, dating, or flying solo, understanding the ins and outs of relationships is key to building strong connections and finding happiness in the world of romance. So go ahead – embrace the adventure, follow your heart, and get ready to write your own epic love story in the pages of Crush Chronicles!

19

SOCIAL MEDIA MANEUVERS: ONLINE ETIQUETTE

Greetings, digital pioneers! So, you've conquered the basics of navigating the online world, from creating accounts to posting cool pics. But wait, there's more! Just like navigating any new territory, venturing into the social media jungle requires a special set of skills: etiquette. This chapter isn't your boring lecture about online safety (although staying safe is pretty cool!). It's about becoming a social media ninja, mastering the art of communication, and leaving a positive digital footprint.

Forget awkward silences and cringe-worthy comments (we've all been there!). This is about becoming a social media ambassador, like a diplomat navigating the intricate world of online interactions. We'll decipher the codes of respect, responsibility, and even privacy, figuring out how to express yourself while keeping it cool and classy. Is it all about perfect grammar and emojis? Nope, it's about being mindful, responsible, and maybe even a little bit witty.

Imagine yourself as a social media archaeologist, venturing into the uncharted territory of your own online presence. You'll be mapping out the different platforms, identifying potential hazards and friendly communities, and piecing together the puzzle of what kind of digital presence you want to create. Is it all about funny memes and epic gaming moments? Or maybe you aspire to share your artistic talents and connect with like-minded individuals? These are the questions, young digital adventurers, that this chapter will help you answer!

Think of growing up as an epic quest, and your social media presence is one of the tools you'll wield. But with great online power comes great responsibility (don't worry, it's more about being thoughtful than wielding superpowers!). This chapter will be your trusty guide, teaching you everything you need to know about navigating the social media landscape, from crafting positive interactions to respecting others' privacy. You'll learn tips for avoiding online drama, using humor responsibly, and even dealing with cyberbullies (because nobody deserves that!).

So, are you ready to unlock the secrets of mindful online interactions and become a social media master? Are you prepared to become a communication champion, an online ambassador, or a champion of respect? Remember, the online world is a powerful tool, and using it wisely and responsibly makes you a positive force in the digital landscape. Now go forth and explore, young padawans of the internet, leaving a trail of awesomeness and good vibes wherever you go!

Now that you're pumped to become a social media superstar, let's dive into the nitty-gritty of online etiquette. Remember, even though it's the virtual world, real people with real feelings exist behind those screens. So, let's treat each other with kindness and respect, just like we would in real life (maybe even cooler, because who doesn't love a good online compliment?).

Think Before You Post:

Remember, once it's online, it's out there forever. So, take a moment to reflect before hitting that "share" button. Would you say it out loud to someone's face? If the answer is "uh oh," maybe rephrase or reconsider.

Respect and Kindness Rule:

Treat everyone online with the same kindness and respect you'd show them in person. No bullying, hate speech, or negativity allowed! We're all here to have fun and connect, not tear each other down.

Privacy Matters:

Be mindful of what you share online, both yours and others. Don't post personal information about yourself or others without permission. Remember, privacy is power, and respecting it shows maturity and responsibility.

Think Twice About Memes and Trends:

Not every meme or trend is created equal. Be mindful of the messages they convey and avoid anything offensive, discriminatory, or hurtful. Remember, humor is subjective, but respect should always be objective.

100

Credit Where Credit is Due:

If you share someone else's content, always give them credit! It's a simple yet respectful way to acknowledge their work and avoid plagiarism. Plus, it makes you look like a responsible digital citizen.

These actions can go a really long way. More than you can imagine.

Action	Why It Matters	Bonus Tip
Think before you post	Avoid regrettable moments and protect your digital footprint.	Reflect on the potential impact of your words and images.
Respect and kindness rule	Create a positive online community and show maturity.	Treat everyone with the same respect you want to receive.
Privacy matters	Protect yourself and others from unwanted exposure.	Share responsibly and avoid posting personal information without permission.
Think twice about memes and trends	Maintain your values and avoid perpetuating negativity.	Choose humor that uplifts and avoids discriminatory or harmful messages.
Credit where credit is due	Show respect for others' work and avoid plagiarism.	Always acknowledge the source of content you share.

Bonus Tips for Online Awesomeness:

Engage Positively:

Comment and like other people's content but do it meaningfully. Leave encouraging comments, ask questions, and have genuine conversations. Avoid spamming or mindless compliments.

Be Mindful of Your Online Language:

Ditch the excessive slang and text-speak when appropriate. Proper grammar and punctuation show you take your online presence seriously, especially in formal settings.

Curate Your Feed:

Follow accounts that inspire, uplift, and make you laugh. Avoid negativity and drama magnets. Remember, your feed reflects your online interests, so make it positive and uplifting.

Take a Break When Needed:

Social media can be overwhelming sometimes. If you feel stressed or anxious, take a break! Disconnect and recharge. Your mental health is more important than online clout.

Remember, being a social media master isn't about chasing likes and followers. It's about using this powerful tool responsibly, spreading positivity, and connecting with others respectfully and meaningfully. So, go forth, young digital citizens, and conquer the online world with your kindness, wit, and positive vibes!

20

FITNESS FUEL: EXERCISE FOR A CHANGING BODY

Hey there, fitness enthusiasts! Whether you're into sports, outdoor adventures, or hitting the gym, understanding how to exercise effectively and safely is key to feeling strong, confident, and energized. So, grab your workout gear and get ready to unleash your inner fitness warrior as we dive into the world of Fitness Fuel!

First, let's talk about why exercise is so important, especially during the tween and teen years. As your body goes through puberty, you're experiencing rapid growth and development, which means your muscles, bones, and organs are all changing and maturing. Regular exercise helps support this growth process, strengthens your muscles and bones, and improves your overall health and well-being.

Now, you might wonder, "What kinds of exercise should I be doing?" Great question! The good news is there are plenty of options to choose from when it comes to staying active. Whether you're into team sports like soccer or basketball, individual activities like swimming or biking, or outdoor adventures like hiking or rock climbing, the key is to find activities that you enjoy and that make you feel good.

Next up, let's talk about the benefits of exercise beyond just physical health. Sure, staying active is great for building strong muscles and bones, improving cardiovascular health, and maintaining a healthy weight – but it's also a powerful tool for boosting your mood, reducing stress, and improving mental clarity and focus. So, the next time you're feeling stressed out or overwhelmed, lace up your sneakers and go for a run – you'll be amazed at how much better you feel afterward!

Now, let's talk about how to create a balanced exercise routine that works for you. The key is to include various activities that target different muscle groups and aspects of fitness. Aim for a mix of cardiovascular exercises to get your heart pumping, strength training to build muscle and bone density, and flexibility exercises to improve your range of motion and prevent injury.

But here's the thing – exercise should never feel like a chore or punishment. It's all about finding activities that you enjoy and that make you feel good. So, if you're not into running or lifting weights, that's totally okay! Get creative and think outside the box – try dancing, yoga, martial arts, or even just playing tag with your friends at the park. The important thing is to keep moving and have fun while doing it!

Fuel Up & Move On: Your Flexible Fitness Routine Checklist

Alright, young explorers, now that you're pumped to move your body, here's a handy checklist to help you create your own personalized fitness routine:

My Daily Movement Goals

Cardio:

Aim for at least 30 minutes of moderate-intensity activity most days of the week. This could be running, biking, swimming, dancing, or even playing tag with friends.

Strength: Do some bodyweight exercises or use light weights 2-3 times a week to build strength and coordination. Push-ups, squats, lunges, and jumping jacks are all great options.

Flexibility:

Stretch gently for 5-10 minutes daily to improve your range of motion and prevent injuries. Yoga, simple stretches, or even reaching for the sky after waking up can help!

Activity Adventure Ideas:

- Teamwork Fun: Join a sports team, play frisbee with friends, or have a family soccer match.

- Solo Missions: Hike in nature, ride a bike, or try a new fitness app for a solo workout.

- Rainy Day Games: Have an indoor dance party, build an obstacle course in your living room, or challenge yourself to some jumping jacks and sit-ups.

- Creative Movement: Put on some music and dance like nobody's watching, invent your own exercise routine, or create a fitness obstacle course in your backyard.

But never exercise without being mindful of your body. Listen to your body when it is tired and cannot go on anymore. This is the age where you have to start trusting your guts and believing in yourself...

Listen to your body:

Take breaks when needed, and don't push yourself too hard.

Safety first:

Always wear appropriate clothing and gear for your chosen activity.

Make it fun!

Choose activities you enjoy and mix things up to keep it interesting.

Celebrate your progress:

Track your achievements and milestones, no matter how small!

This is just a starting point, young adventurer! With this checklist and a little creativity, you can build a flexible fitness routine that fuels your body, mind, and spirit.

Now, let's address the elephant in the room – puberty and body image. As your body changes and matures, you might start to feel self-conscious or insecure about your appearance. But here's the truth – exercise is about so much more than just how you look. It's about feeling strong, confident, and capable in your own skin, regardless of what you see in the mirror. So, focus on how exercise makes you feel – strong, powerful, and unstoppable – and let that motivate you to keep moving forward.

Let's end this chapter with a rough image of how an easy exercise routine can look like:

Day	Cardio Blast (30 min)	Strength Mission (20 min)	Flexibility Flow (10 min)	Bonus Adventure
Monday	Run around the block with friends	Push-ups, squats, lunges	Cat-cow poses, hamstring stretches	Invent a "superhero training" obstacle course in the backyard
Tuesday	Bike ride with family	Planks, sit-ups, wall climbers	Downward-facing dog, arm circles	Dance party to your favorite music
Wednesday	Soccer game with classmates	Jumping jacks, high knees, butt kicks	Yoga poses for kids	Climb a tree (safely!)
Thursday	Swim laps at the pool	Monkey bars, pull-ups (assisted if needed)	Butterfly stretches, side bends	Build a fort and crawl through it
Friday	Parkour challenge in the backyard	Shadow boxing, wall sits	Head rolls, shoulder stretches	Play tag or hide-and-seek
Weekend	Hike in nature with family	Obstacle course at a local park	Partner stretches with a friend	Play a sport you love

21
FUELING GROWTH: NUTRITION ESSENTIALS

As your body goes through puberty and experiences rapid growth and development, fueling yourself with the nutrients you need to thrive is more important than ever. So, grab a plate and get ready to dive into the delicious world of Fueling Growth!

First, let's talk about why nutrition is so important during the tween and teen years. As your body grows and changes, it needs a steady supply of vitamins, minerals, protein, carbohydrates, and healthy fats to support this growth process. Proper nutrition provides the energy you need to fuel your activities and adventures and plays a crucial role in maintaining healthy bones, muscles, organs, and hormones.

Now, you might be wondering, "What exactly should I be eating?" Great question! The key to a healthy diet is balance and variety. Aim to fill your plate with colorful fruits and vegetables, whole grains, lean proteins, and healthy fats. Think of your meals as a chance to create a rainbow of nutrients – the more colors, the better!

Next up, let's talk about the importance of hydration. Staying hydrated is essential for maintaining optimal health and performance, especially when you're active and sweating up a storm. Aim to drink plenty of water throughout the day, and consider adding in some hydrating foods like watermelon, cucumbers, and oranges to help boost your hydration levels even further.

Let's address the elephant in the room – junk food and sugary treats. While it's okay to indulge in the occasional treat or snack, it's important to remember that these foods should be enjoyed in moderation. Instead of reaching for potato chips or candy bars, try snacking on nutrient-rich foods like nuts, seeds, yogurt, or fresh fruit to keep your energy levels and cravings at bay.

But here's the thing – healthy eating isn't about deprivation or strict rules. It's about finding a balance that works for you and your body. So, don't be afraid to enjoy your favorite foods in moderation and listen to your body's hunger and fullness cues. By practicing mindful eating and paying attention to how different foods make you feel, you can learn to fuel your body in a way that nourishes and satisfies you from the inside out.

Now, let's talk about meal planning and preparation. Planning and preparing your meals ahead of time is a great way to ensure that you have healthy options on hand when hunger strikes. Try setting aside some time each week to plan out your meals, make a grocery list, and prep some ingredients in advance – whether it's chopping veggies, cooking grains, or grilling chicken. With some foresight and organization, eating healthy can be easy, convenient, and delicious!

It's time to look at the bigger picture – the role of food in your overall health and well-being. Food is more than just fuel – it's also a source of pleasure, joy, and connection. So, don't forget to savor your meals, enjoy the flavors and textures, and share your love of food with others. Whether you're cooking a meal with your family, sharing a picnic with friends, or trying a new recipe on your own, food can nourish your body and feed your soul.

Eating a balanced and varied diet is key to fueling your body for growth, activity, and overall well-being. The following table is just a starting point, so don't be afraid to experiment and find what works best for you!

Food Group	What It Does	Examples	Tips for Young Champions
Fruits and Vegetables:	Packed with vitamins, minerals, and fiber for energy, growth, and overall health.	Berries, citrus fruits, leafy greens, broccoli, carrots, and sweet potatoes	Choose a variety of colors and types for different nutrients. Aim for at least five servings a day.
Whole Grains:	Provide sustained energy and fiber for good digestion and heart health.	Brown rice, quinoa, whole-wheat bread, oatmeal, popcorn	Opt for whole grains over refined options whenever possible.

Lean Protein:	Essential for building and repairing muscles, bones, and other body tissues.	Chicken, fish, beans, lentils, tofu, yogurt	Choose lean cuts of meat and avoid processed options. Include plant-based protein sources.
Healthy Fats:	Support brain function, growth, and absorption of vitamins.	Avocados, nuts, seeds, olive oil, and fatty fish	Choose healthy fats over saturated and trans fats found in fried foods and processed snacks.
Dairy (or Dairy Alternatives):	Rich in calcium for strong bones and teeth, and often fortified with vitamin D.	Milk, cheese, yogurt, plant-based milk with added calcium and vitamin D	Choose low-fat or fat-free options and limit sugary yogurts and drinks.
Hydration:	Crucial for all bodily functions, including digestion, temperature regulation, and brain function.	Water, unsweetened tea, milk, and fruit-infused water	Drink plenty of water throughout the day, especially during exercise and hot weather.

Now, let's talk about some specific nutrients that are particularly important for your growing body. First up, let's talk about calcium. Calcium is essential for building strong bones and teeth and plays a crucial role in bone growth and development during puberty. Aim to include plenty of calcium-rich foods in your diet, such as dairy products like milk, yogurt, and cheese, as well as leafy green vegetables like kale and broccoli.

Next, let's talk about protein. Protein is the building block of muscles, tissues, and organs, and it's essential for supporting growth and development during puberty. Aim to include a source of protein in each of your meals and snacks, such as lean meats, poultry, fish, eggs, tofu, beans, and nuts. And don't forget about the power of plant-based protein sources like quinoa, lentils, and chickpeas – they're just as nutritious and delicious as their animal-based counterparts!

Now, let's talk about carbohydrates. Carbohydrates are your body's primary energy source, and they're especially important for fueling your activities and adventures as a growing teen. Aim to include a mix of complex carbohydrates – like whole grains, fruits, and vegetables – and simple carbohydrates – like sugars found in fruits, dairy products, and sweet treats – in your diet to provide sustained energy throughout the day.

And finally, let's talk about fats. Healthy fats are essential for brain health, hormone production, and nutrient absorption, and they're an important part of a balanced diet. Aim to include sources of healthy fats in your meals and snacks, such as avocados, nuts, seeds, olive oil, and fatty fish like salmon and tuna. And don't forget about the importance of omega-3 fatty acids – found in fish oil, flaxseed, and walnuts – for supporting brain health and cognitive function.

Nutrition is the cornerstone of a healthy and vibrant life, especially during the tween and teen years. By fueling your body with a balanced and varied diet rich in essential nutrients like calcium, protein, carbohydrates, and healthy fats, you can support your growth and development, boost your energy levels, and feel your best from the inside out. So go ahead – fill your plate with colorful, nutrient-rich foods, and get ready to fuel your growth with Fueling Growth!

Important Reminders:

- Limit sugary drinks, processed snacks, and fried foods.

- Read food labels and choose options with lower sodium and added sugars.

- Involve your family in meal planning and cooking to learn healthy habits together.

- Listen to your body and eat until you're comfortably full, not stuffed.

- Make healthy eating fun and explore new recipes with friends and family.

22

SLEEP LIKE A BOSS: REST FOR THE ACTIVE TEEN

Sleep is like a superpower – it rejuvenates your body, sharpens your mind, and sets you up for success in everything you do. So, let's dive into the wonderful world of sleep and learn how to catch those Z's like a boss!

Let's talk about why sleep is so important, especially during the tween and teen years. Sleep plays a crucial role in supporting this process as your body goes through puberty and experiences rapid growth and development. During sleep, your body repairs and rebuilds tissues releases growth hormones and consolidates memories – all essential functions for a healthy body and mind.

Now, you might wonder, "How much sleep do I need?" Great question! The answer depends on your age and individual needs, but most experts recommend that teens aim for around 8-10 hours of sleep per night. Yep, you heard that right – a solid 8-10 hours of shut-eye each night is essential for feeling your best and performing your best, both physically and mentally.

Next up, let's talk about the benefits of getting enough sleep. Not only does sleep help you feel rested and refreshed, but it improves your mood, boosts your immune system, enhances your memory and concentration, and even helps regulate your appetite and metabolism. In other words, sleep is like a magic potion that helps you look, feel, and perform your best in everything you do.

But here's the thing – getting enough sleep isn't just about quantity; it's also about quality. That means creating a sleep-friendly environment that promotes relaxation and restfulness. Keep your bedroom cool, dark, and quiet, and invest in a comfortable mattress and pillows that support your body and help you drift off to dreamland.

Now, let's talk about some tips for improving your sleep hygiene and getting the most out of your nightly slumber. First off, establish a regular sleep schedule by going to bed and waking up at the same time every day – yes, even on weekends! This helps regulate your body's internal clock and makes it easier to fall asleep and wake up feeling refreshed.

Next, let's talk about winding down before bed. Give yourself at least an hour before bedtime to relax and unwind – that means powering down screens, dimming the lights, and engaging in calming activities like reading, journaling, or taking a warm bath.

Avoid stimulating activities like playing video games or watching action-packed movies, as these can make it harder to fall asleep.

Time for the serious talk– caffeine and electronics. Yep, your favorite energy drinks and late-night scrolling sessions might wreak havoc on your sleep quality. Caffeine can interfere with your body's natural sleep-wake cycle and make it harder to fall asleep. At the same time, the blue light emitted by screens can suppress the production of melatonin – the hormone that regulates sleep. So, limit your intake of caffeine and screen time, especially in the hours leading up to bedtime, to ensure a restful night's sleep.

And finally, let's talk about the importance of listening to your body. If you're feeling tired or sluggish during the day, that's your body's way of telling you that you need more sleep. So, don't ignore those signals – prioritize rest and relaxation, and make sleep a non-negotiable part of your self-care routine. Your body and mind will thank you for it!

Sleep is essential to health and well-being, especially for active and growing teens. By prioritizing quality rest, establishing a regular sleep schedule, and creating a sleep-friendly environment, you can unlock the full potential of your mind and body and wake up feeling like a boss every single day. So go ahead – slip into your favorite pajamas, snuggle up under the covers, and get ready to sleep like a boss!

23

STRESS LESS: COPING STRATEGIES FOR TOUGH TIMES

Life can throw some curveballs your way, but with the right coping strategies, you can conquer stress like a pro and emerge stronger than ever. So, let's roll up our sleeves and dive into the world of Stress Less!

First off, let's unpack what stress truly means. It's like your body's built-in alarm system, ready to ping when demands or threats arise. But sometimes, that alarm system can go into overdrive, leaving you feeling overwhelmed, anxious, and exhausted.

Now, you might be pondering, "What exactly triggers stress?" Well, stress can be triggered by a myriad of factors – from major life events like moving to a new school or dealing with a family crisis to the everyday grind of exams, friendships, and extracurricular activities. Recognizing your triggers is key to developing healthy coping mechanisms to manage them effectively.

Next up, the subtle signs and symptoms of stress. They can vary from person to person, but some common indicators include feeling irritable or moody, struggling with concentration or decision-making, experiencing changes in appetite or sleep patterns, and feeling overwhelmed or hopeless. Identifying these signs is the first step in addressing them head-on.

Now, let's delve into some coping strategies for tackling stress head-on. First, let's discuss the power of relaxation techniques. Whether it's deep breathing, meditation, progressive muscle relaxation, or visualization exercises, finding ways to relax your body and mind can be a game-changer in reducing stress and fostering a sense of calm and balance.

Next, let's emphasize the importance of staying connected. When stress hits hard, retreating and isolating yourself can be tempting. But reaching out to friends, family, or trusted adults can provide invaluable support and perspective during tough times. Having someone to talk to, seek advice, or simply lean on can make all the difference.

Moving forward, let's reflect on the power of perspective. When you're knee-deep in stress, negative thoughts can spiral out of control. Taking a step back and looking at the bigger picture can help reframe challenges as temporary and manageable. Shifting your focus from what you can't control to what you can empowers you to face stressors with a renewed sense of resilience.

Lastly, let's emphasize the importance of self-care. When stress weighs heavy, prioritizing your physical and emotional well-being is non-negotiable. That means nourishing your body with nutritious foods, prioritizing sleep, engaging in regular exercise, and carving out time for activities that bring you joy and fulfillment. Remember – taking care of yourself isn't selfish; it's vital to resilience and well-being.

Stress may be an inevitable part of life, but with the right coping strategies, you can confidently navigate its tumultuous waters. By practicing relaxation techniques, fostering connections, gaining perspective, and prioritizing self-care, you can build resilience and weather any storm that comes your way. So go ahead – take a deep breath, reach out for support, and remember that you have the power to Stress Less and thrive amidst adversity!

24

HEART-TO-HEART TALKS WITH PARENTS

Remember all that cool stuff we discussed in the last chapters? Growing bodies, changing voices, and how everything's part of this awesome adventure called puberty? Well, guess what? Sometimes, even on this grand adventure, things can get confusing or even scary. That's okay! Everyone feels that way sometimes, even grown-ups (shhh, don't tell them I said that!).

When things get rough, when you have questions or worries, or just need someone to listen, guess who's always got your back? Your incredible parents! Remember, they were once kids, too, going through the same changes you are now. They might not have all the answers, but they have a shoulder to lean on and a listening ear waiting just for you.

Now, I know talking to parents can feel like climbing Mount Everest in your pajamas. Your stomach might do flip-flops, your voice might squeak, and you might worry they'll think you're silly. But trust me, they won't! They want you to talk to them, and here's why:

They love you:

More than pizza, video games, and even their favorite socks (probably). And like any superhero loves their sidekick, they want to be there for you through thick and thin, weird questions and all.

They understand (more than you think):

Maybe not everything, but they remember what it was like to be your age. They might even share some funny (or embarrassing!) stories about their growing-up days.

They can help:

Whether it's a confusing feeling, a worry about changes, or just need a hug, your parents can offer advice and support or simply be there to listen. Sometimes, just talking things out can make a big difference!

So, how do you start this heart-to-heart? Here are some tips:

1. **Pick the right time:** Don't ambush them when they're stressed or rushing out the door. Look for a relaxed moment, maybe after dinner or while watching a movie together.

2. **Start small:** You don't have to unload everything at once. Begin with something simple, like, "Hey, Mom/Dad, I have a question about..."

3. **Be honest:** Don't be afraid to say what's really on your mind, even if it feels silly or embarrassing. Remember, they love you no matter what.

4. **Listen to them too:** They might have some wise words, funny stories, or simply offer a reassuring hug.

Remember, communication is a two-way street. Talking to your parents doesn't make you weak; it makes you strong. It shows them you trust them, and it opens the door to a deeper connection and understanding. So, take a deep breath, gather your courage, and remember, they're your biggest cheerleaders on this amazing journey called growing up!

And hey, if things still feel tough, remember you're not alone. Talk to a trusted teacher, counselor, or even a cool older sibling. There are many people who care and want to help you navigate this exciting, sometimes confusing, adventure called puberty.

Breaking the Ice:

Okay, you're ready to talk, but how do you even start? Here are some icebreakers to get the conversation flowing:

Start with a question: "Hey, Mom/Dad, I was wondering what puberty was like for you?" Hearing their experiences might put yours in perspective and make things feel less alien.

Talk about something specific: "Lately, my voice has been cracking a lot, and it's kinda embarrassing. Is that normal?" Focusing on a specific concern can ease into a bigger conversation.

Use a book or website as a springboard: "I was reading this book about puberty, and it talked about mood swings. Do you think that's why I've been feeling grumpy lately?" Using a shared resource can create a comfortable talking point.

Remember, you don't have to be perfect. Stumble, stammer, it's all part of the process. Your parents will appreciate your effort and happily answer your questions, even if they're a little awkward.

Troubleshooting:

Sometimes, even with the best intentions, things don't go as planned. Don't give up if your parents seem dismissive, embarrassed, or uncomfortable! Here are some tips:

- Try again later: Maybe they were having a tough day. Pick another time when they seem more relaxed and receptive.

- Seek another trusted adult: If talking to your parents still feels challenging, reach out to another adult you trust, like an aunt, uncle, teacher, or counselor. They can offer support and guidance.

- Write it down: If talking feels too overwhelming, try writing down your questions and concerns and sharing them with your parents.

Remember, you're not alone: Many kids feel nervous about talking to their parents about puberty. But trust me, it's worth it! Open communication builds a stronger bond, leads to better understanding, and helps you navigate this exciting, sometimes confusing, time in your life.

After a good heart-to-heart, thank your parents for listening. Let them know it means a lot to you and that you appreciate their support. This strengthens communication and encourages further openness in the future.

So, go forth, young champion, and conquer your communication fears! Remember, talking to your parents is a sign of strength, not weakness. With a little courage and these tips, you can embark on an amazing journey of understanding, support, and growth, both with yourself and with the incredible people who love you the most. Now, go out there and have those awesome heart-to-heart talks!

25

LOOKING AHEAD: THE ROAD TO ADULTHOOD

As you stand at the threshold of adolescence, gazing out into the vast expanse of the future, it's natural to feel a whirlwind of emotions – excitement, uncertainty, anticipation, and perhaps a touch of apprehension. The road to adulthood is a winding path, full of twists and turns, triumphs, and challenges, but it's also a journey ripe with possibilities and opportunities for growth. So, let's embark on a voyage of self-discovery as we peer into the horizon and explore what lies ahead on the road to adulthood.

First and foremost, let's reflect on the concept of adulthood itself. What does it mean to be an adult? Is it simply a matter of reaching a certain age, or is it something more profound – a state of mind, a sense of responsibility, a commitment to self-discovery and personal growth? As you ponder these questions, remember that adulthood is not a destination but a journey, and the path you choose to walk is uniquely yours to define.

You need to contemplate some milestones and transitions that mark the journey into adulthood. From graduating high school and pursuing higher education or entering the workforce to forging new relationships, exploring your passions, and finding your place in the world, each step brings its own challenges and growth opportunities. Embrace these milestones with an open heart and a spirit of curiosity, knowing that each experience is a stepping stone on the path to becoming the person you were meant to be.

Next, let's consider some of the skills and qualities that are essential for navigating the road to adulthood with grace and resilience. Adaptability, resilience, perseverance, and a growth mindset are just some traits that will serve you well as you journey through life's twists and turns. Cultivate these qualities within yourself, and you'll find that no challenge is too great and no obstacle too daunting to overcome.

Now, let's discuss the importance of setting goals and mapping your path forward. What are your dreams, your aspirations, and your ambitions for the future? Take the time to envision the life you want to live, and then set concrete goals and action plans to help you turn your dreams into reality. Whether it's pursuing a career you're passionate about, traveling the world, starting a family, or making a difference in your community, the sky's the limit when it comes to charting your course in life.

But here's the thing – the road to adulthood is not always smooth sailing. You'll encounter setbacks, challenges, and detours that may test your resolve and shake your confidence. But remember – it's not the challenges themselves that define you, but how you respond to them. Embrace adversity as an opportunity for growth, learn from your mistakes, and keep moving forward with courage and determination.

The road to adulthood is a journey of self-discovery, growth, and transformation. As you navigate the twists and turns of life, remember to embrace each experience with an open heart and a spirit of curiosity, knowing that every challenge you face and every milestone you reach brings you one step closer to becoming the person you were meant to be. So go ahead – embrace the journey, seize the opportunities, and let your dreams light the way as you embark on the adventure of a lifetime.

CONCLUSION

And just like that, dear readers, we've reached the end of our adventure together. But fear not, for your journey is far from over! As you close the pages of "A Guide for Boys About Changing Bodies," remember that the story of your body is an ongoing saga, filled with twists, turns, and unexpected discoveries.

Throughout this book, we've explored the mysteries of puberty, from the first signs of change to the triumphant emergence of newfound confidence. We've laughed together, learned together, and maybe even cringed a little together – because, let's face it, puberty can be a rollercoaster ride of emotions and experiences.

But through it all, one thing remains constant: you are not alone. Every boy embarks on this journey of self-discovery, facing similar challenges and triumphs along the way. So, whether you're grappling with body hair, battling breakouts, or wrestling with new emotions, know that there's a whole community of fellow adventurers cheering you on.

Until we meet again, fellow adventurers, may your adventures be wild, your discoveries be thrilling, and your hearts be forever young. Farewell for now, but remember – the best is yet to come!

SPECIAL BONUS

Want this bonus book for free?

SKILLS and be the first to claim a free
download of our upcoming releases.

Scan the
QR CODE

**Join
Today!**

THANK YOU

Thank you for choosing our resource to support your child's growth; it means so much to us.

If you could take a moment to share your thoughts on Amazon or Goodreads.com, it would mean a lot to us and be a great help to other parents searching for trusted resources. Thank you.

Want to dive into the literary world before anyone else? Then join our Book Launch Club! As a club member, you'll be offered the opportunity to receive advanced copies of our upcoming releases directly to your inbox. All we ask is for you to leave honest reviews on Amazon.com and Goodreads.com. Your honest feedback will contribute to the book's success and help fellow readers make informed choices.

For more information on joining Skilled Fun's Book Launch Club skilledfun.com/book-launch-club or simply scan our QR CODE

Made in the USA
Monee, IL
09 June 2025

19092729R00075